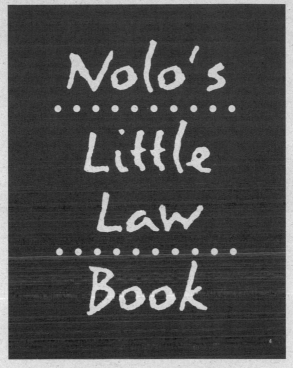

Nolo's Little Law Book

ANSWERS TO EVERYDAY LEGAL QUESTIONS

by The Editors of Nolo Press

Edited by Shae Irving

NOLO PRESS ⚖ BERKELEY

Your Responsibility When Using a Self-help Law Book

We've done our best to give you useful and accurate information in this book. But laws and procedures change frequently and are subject to differing interpretations. If you want legal advice backed by a guarantee, see a lawyer. If you use this book, it's your responsibility to make sure that the facts and general advice contained in it are applicable to your situation.

To help you stay current, Nolo Press provides an update service in its quarterly newspaper, the *Nolo News*. See the inside back cover for information on how you can get a free two-year subscription to the *Nolo News*.

Printing History

First Edition	MARCH 1996
Editors	SHAE IRVING, ROBIN LEONARD, MARY RANDOLPH
Design	JACKIE MANCUSO & NANCY ERB
Proofreading	ROBERT WELLS
Printing	DELTA LITHOGRAPH

Printed on 100% recycled paper,
with 25-35% post-consumer waste.
Cover coating is water based

FROM THE PUBLISHER

Nolo Press is proud to be celebrating its 25th anniversary this year. To thank our customers and friends for supporting and sustaining us over the last quarter century, we're giving away 100,000 copies of this little book.

Twenty-five years ago, almost all Americans believed the legal profession's favorite propaganda line: If you represent yourself, you have a fool for a client. In that climate, it took a brave spirit to pick up a self-help law book from Nolo Press, a tiny and unknown publishing company whose headquarters were a couple of rooms in a Berkeley, California, brown-shingle house.

Just imagine what it must have been like for a person with no legal training to enter a courtroom in the early 1970s armed with only a copy of one of Nolo's first two books, the *California Tenants' Handbook* (now called *Tenants' Rights*) or *How to Do Your Own Divorce in California*. Almost surely the court clerks were hostile, the judge unbelieving and the lawyer for the other side gleeful.

Undoubtedly, some of those first self-helpers were intimidated. But lots of them determinedly exercised their fundamental democratic right to use our legal system without paying a lawyer to get them into the courthouse. And as they continued to do so in ever-increasing numbers throughout the 1970s, the "lawyers only" legal system of the time grew a little less hostile to those who sought to represent themselves. By 1980, the word had spread: handling your own legal matters could be safe, effective and affordable.

Before long it dawned on the more progressive lawyers, judges and court administrators that the American people were not only in their courthouses to stay, but were beginning to demand that courthouse rules, legal procedures and even the law itself be made as user-friendly as possible. Far too reluctantly and far too hesitantly, the mainstream legal profession began to respond.

Today, common-sense measures that Nolo advocated 20 years ago—measures that lawyers dismissed or scoffed at—have at long last started to appear. Many courts now issue fill-in-the-blank forms and instructions to simplify the paperwork for routine court matters. Some states have adopted "Plain English" laws, encouraging (with mixed results) laws to be written in everyday language. A few courthouses have opened Self-Help Centers to guide non-lawyers. And perhaps most important, many judges and court staffers have adopted a respectful attitude toward people who cannot afford or choose not to hire a lawyer to speak for them.

Throughout this exciting quarter-century, we at Nolo Press have continued to publish the most accurate and up-to-date self-help law materials we could. Along the way Nolo grew from a company of a few part-time workers to one with more than 80 employees and a roster of more than 100 books, software, audiotapes and videotapes. From California-only books, we've expanded across the country and more recently, into cyberspace: we now have our own Self-Help Law Centers online (see the inside of the front cover). All told, we estimate that Nolo has sold about five million copies of its materials. If every book saved someone $200 in legal fees (a conservative estimate in most cases), that's $1 billion that people didn't have to spend on lawyers.

But the real credit belongs to the people who clutched Nolo books and marched into courthouses across the country. Their quiet persistence and sheer numbers have forced enormous, and enormously good, changes in the legal system. We dedicate this book to them.

Ralph Warner
Berkeley, California
January 1996

ABOUT THIS BOOK

Whether we like it or not, the law touches our personal lives in many ways each day. We may not think much about the laws that affect us as we carry out simple tasks such as driving a car, making a telephone call or buying milk at the corner grocery store. But every now and again, we're sure to need an answer to a common legal question that arises in the course of daily life:

What can I do about my noisy neighbor?

What are my rights if I'm fired from my job?

Do I really need to make a will?

And so on.

This book provides answers to frequently asked questions about 25 subjects you might encounter in your personal life—topics that range from buying a house to getting a divorce, from paying your debts to resolving a dispute in small claims court. Obviously, a book this size can't answer every question on a particular subject, so we've answered some of the most common ones to get you started. At the end of each section, you'll find a list of Nolo and non-Nolo resources you can use to get more information about a particular subject. (A catalog of all Nolo publications is in the back of the book.)

As part of our 25th anniversary celebration, this book is our gift to you—a way of saying thanks for making Nolo possible by supporting our commitment to making the law accessible to all.

TABLE OF CONTENTS

1. Neighbors

Years ago, problems between neighbors were resolved informally, perhaps with the help of a third person respected by both sides. These days, neighbors—who may not know each other well, if at all—are quicker to head for court. Usually, of course, lawsuits only exacerbate bad feelings and cost everyone money, and the courthouse should be the place of last, not first, resort. But knowing the legal ground rules is important; you may prevent small disputes from turning into big ones.

1. How can I find the exact boundaries of my property?

You can hire a licensed land surveyor to survey the property and place official markers on the boundary lines. A simple survey usually costs about $500; if no survey has been done for a long time, or the maps are unreliable and conflicting, be prepared to spend up to $1,000.

2. My neighbor and I don't want to pay a surveyor. Can't we just build a fence and agree that it marks the boundary?

You and the neighbor can decide where you want the line to be, and then make it so by signing deeds that describe the boundary. If you have a mortgage on the property, consult an attorney for help in drawing up the deeds. You may need to get the permission of the mortgage holder before you give your neighbor even a tiny piece of the land.

Once you have signed a deed, you should record (file) it at the county land records office, usually called the County Recorder's Office, Land Registry Office or something similar. Deeds are discussed in more detail in the third section of this book.

3. What can I do if a neighbor starts using my property?

If a neighbor starts to build on what you think is your property, do something immediately. If the neighbor's encroachment is minor—for instance, a small fence in the wrong place—you may think you shouldn't worry. But you're wrong. When you try to sell your house, a title company might refuse to issue insurance because the neighbor is on your land.

Also, if you don't act promptly, you could lose part of your property. When one person uses another's land for a long enough time, he can gain a legal right to continue to do so and, in some circumstances, gain ownership of the property.

Talk to your neighbor right away. Most likely, a mistake has been made because of a conflicting description in the neighbor's deed or just a mistaken assumption about the boundary line. If your neighbor is hostile and insists on proceeding, state that you will sue if necessary. Then send a firm letter—or have a lawyer send one on his or her letterhead. If the building doesn't stop, waste no time in having a lawyer get a judge's order to temporarily stop the neighbor until you can bring a civil lawsuit for trespass before the judge.

4. Most of a big oak tree hangs over my yard, but the trunk is on the neighbor's property. Who owns the tree?

Your neighbor. It is accepted law in all states that a tree whose trunk stands wholly on the land of one person belongs to that person.

If the trunk stands partly on the land of two or more people, it is called a boundary tree, and in most cases it belongs to all the property owners. All the owners are responsible for caring for the tree, and one co-owner may not remove a healthy tree without the other owners' permission.

5. Can I trim the branches of the neighbors' tree that hang over my yard?

You have the legal right to trim tree branches up to the property line. But you may not go onto the neighbor's property or destroy the tree itself.

6. My neighbor dug up his yard, and in the process killed a tree that's just on my side of the property line. Am I entitled to compensation for the tree?

Yes. The basic rule is that someone who cuts down, removes or hurts a tree without permission owes the tree's owner money to compensate for the harm done. You can sue to enforce that right—but you probably won't have to, once you tell your neighbor what the law is.

7. My neighbor's tree looks like it's going to fall on my house any day now. What should I do?

You can trim back branches to your property line, but that may not solve the problem if you're worried about the whole tree coming down.

City governments often step in to take care of, or make the owner take care of, dangerous trees. Some cities have ordinances that prohibit maintaining any dangerous condition—including a hazardous tree—on private property. To enforce such an ordinance, the city can demand that the owner remove the tree or pay a fine. Some cities will even remove such a tree for the owner. To check on your city's laws and policies, call the city attorney's office.

You might also get help from a utility company, if the tree threatens its equipment. For example, a phone company will trim a tree that hangs menacingly over its lines.

If you don't get help from these sources, and the neighbor refuses to take action, you can sue. The legal theory is that the dangerous tree is a "nuisance" because it is unreasonable for the owner to keep it and it interferes with your use and enjoyment of your property. You can ask the court to order the owner to prune or remove the tree. You'll have to sue in regular court (not small claims court) and have proof that the tree really does pose a danger to you.

8. My neighbor's trees have grown so much that they block my once sweeping view. Do I have any legal right to have them cut back?

Probably not. In this situation, you have no legal right to your old view unless it is granted by a local ordinance or subdivision rule.

If you do live where a view rule is in force, you may have the right to sue a neighbor whose trees grow and block your view. But first, you must ask the neighbor to cut back the tree. And if your case does go to court, the judge will weigh several factors: your view, the health of the trees, and the importance of the trees to the owner.

9. My neighbor's dog barks all the time and it's driving me crazy. What can I do?

Usually, problems with barking dogs can be resolved without resorting to police or courts. Here are the steps to take when you're losing patience (or sleep) over a neighbor's noisy dog:

    1. Ask your neighbor to keep the dog quiet. Sometimes owners are blissfully unaware that there's a problem. If the dog barks for hours every day—but only when it's left alone—the owner may not know that you're being driven crazy. Also, if you do eventually end up in court, a judge will be more sympathetic if you made at least some effort to work things out first. If you can establish some rapport with the neighbor, try to agree on specific actions to alleviate the problem: for example, that your neighbor will take the dog to obedience school, or that the dog will be kept inside after 10 pm. After you agree on a plan, set a date to talk again in a couple of weeks.

2. Try mediation, which provides a safe, structured way for neighbors to talk. Mediators, both professional and volunteers, are trained to listen to both sides, identify problems, keep everyone focused on the real issues and suggest compromises. A mediator won't make a decision for you, but will help you and your neighbor agree on a resolution.

Many cities have community mediation groups which train volunteers to mediate disputes in their own neighborhoods. Or ask for a referral from:

- The small claims court clerk's office.
- The local district attorney's office—the consumer complaint division, if there is one.
- Radio or television stations that offer help with consumer problems.
- State or local bar associations.

3. Look up the law. In some places, barking dogs are covered by a specific state or local ordinance. If there's no law aimed specifically at dogs, a general nuisance or noise ordinance makes the owner responsible. Local law may forbid loud noise after 10 pm, for example, or prohibit any "unreasonable" noise. And someone who allows a dog to bark after numerous warnings from police may be arrested for disturbing the peace.

To find out what the law is where you live, go to a law library and check the state statutes and city or county ordinances yourself. Look in the index under "noise," "dogs," "animals" or "nuisance." Or call the local animal control agency or city attorney.

4. Ask animal control authorities to enforce local noise laws. Be persistent. Some cities have special programs to handle dog complaints.

5. Call the police, if you think a criminal law is being violated. Generally, police aren't too interested in barking dog problems. And summoning a police cruiser to a neighbor's house obviously will not improve your already-strained relations. But if nothing else works, and the relationship with your neighbor is shot anyway, give the police a try.

10. Do I have any legal recourse against a noisy neighbor?

You bet. The most effective weapon you have to maintain your peace and quiet is your local noise ordinance. Almost every community prohibits excessive, unnecessary and unreasonable noise, and police enforce these laws.

Most laws designate certain "quiet hours"—for example, from 10 pm to 7 am on weekdays, and until 8 or 9 am on weekends. So running a power mower may be perfectly acceptable at 10 am on Saturday, but not at 7 am. Many towns also have decibel level noise limits. When a neighbor complains, they measure the noise with electronic equipment. To find out what your town's noise ordinance says, ask at the public library or the city attorney's office.

If your neighbor keeps disturbing you, you can also sue, and ask the court for money damages or to order the neighbor to stop the noise ("abate the nuisance," in legal terms). For money damages alone, you can use small claims court. For a court order telling somebody to stop doing something, you'll have to sue in regular court.

Of course, what you really want is for the nuisance to stop. But getting a small claims court to order your neighbor to pay you money can be amazingly effective. And suing in small claims court is easy, inexpensive and doesn't require a lawyer.

Noise that is excessive and deliberate may also be in violation of state criminal laws against disturbing the peace or disorderly conduct. This means that, in very extreme circumstances, the police can arrest your neighbor. Usually, these offenses are punishable by fines or short jail sentences.

11. The neighbor in the apartment next to mine is very noisy. Isn't the landlord supposed to keep tenants quiet?

In addition to the other remedies all neighbors have, you have another arrow in your quiver: you can lean on the landlord to quiet the neighbor. Standard rental and lease agreements contain a clause entitled "Quiet Enjoyment." This clause gives tenants the right to occupy their apartments in peace, and also imposes upon them the responsibility not to disturb their neighbors. It's the landlord's job to enforce both sides of this bargain.

If the neighbor's stereo is keeping you up every night, the tenants are probably violating the rental agreement, and could be evicted. Especially if several neighbors complain, the landlord will probably order the tenant to comply with the lease or face eviction.

For More Help

Neighbor Law: Fences, Trees, Boundaries and Noise, by Cora Jordan (Nolo Press), explains laws that affect neighbors and shows how to resolve common disputes without lawsuits.

Dog Law, by Mary Randolph (Nolo Press), is a guide to the laws that affect dog owners and their neighbors.

2. Buying a House

Buying a house is an exciting, but often stressful, event. Here are some questions and answers designed to take some of the mystery out of this complex process.

1. I'm a first-time home buyer. Is there any easy way to determine how much house I can afford?

As a broad generalization, most people can afford to purchase a house worth about three times their total (gross) annual income, assuming a 20% down payment and a moderate amount of other long-term debts, such as a car loan or student loans. With no other debts, you can probably afford a house worth up to four or even five times your annual income.

The most accurate way to determine how much house you can afford is to total up your monthly principal and interest payments plus one-twelfth of your yearly bill for property and homeowner's insurance. Now compare that to your gross monthly income. Lenders normally want you to make all monthly housing payments with 28%–33% of your monthly income—the percentage depends on the amount of your down payment, the interest rate on the type of mortgage you want, your credit history, the level of your long-term debts and other factors. A bank or other lender can give you the paperwork you need to determine how much house you can afford.

2. How can I find the best home loan or mortgage?

Many entities, including banks, credit unions, savings and loans, insurance companies and mortgage bankers make home loans. Some lenders work statewide; others specialize in narrow geographical areas, types of housing or types of mortgages. Lenders and terms change frequently as new companies appear, old ones merge and market conditions fluctuate. Fortunately, mortgage rates and fees are usually published in the real estate sections of metropolitan newspapers, and are increasingly available through commercial online services. Also, because many types of home loans are standardized to comply with rules established by the Federal National Mortgage Association (Fannie Mae), a quasi-governmental corporation that purchases a large number of loans from lenders, comparison shopping is not difficult. You can also work with a loan broker, someone who specializes in matching house buyers and appropriate mortgage lenders, normally collecting their fee from the lender.

You may also be eligible for a government-guaranteed loan, offered by the Federal Housing Administration or the U.S. Department of Veterans Affairs, or a loan from a state or local housing agency. These loans usually have low down payment requirements and sometimes offer better-than-market interest rates as well.

Finally, don't forget private sources of mortgage money—parents, other relatives, friends or even the seller of the house you want to buy. Borrowing money privately is usually the most cost-efficient mortgage of all.

3. What's the difference between a fixed and adjustable rate mortgage?

With a fixed rate mortgage, the interest rate and the amount you pay each month remain the same over the entire mortgage term, traditionally 15, 20 or 30 years. With an adjustable rate mortgage (ARM), the interest rate fluctuates according to the interest rates in the economy. Initial interest rates of ARMs are often substantially lower than for fixed rate mortgages. Typically these "teaser" rates last only a few months, at which point ARM interest rates move closer to, but still usually below, comparable fixed rate mortgages. After that, if general interest rates go up or down, so too will ARM rates. To avoid constant and drastic fluctuations, ARMs typically regulate (cap) how much and how often the interest rate and/or payments can change in a year and over the life of the loan.

A number of variations are available for adjustable rate mortgages, including hybrids that change from a fixed to an adjustable rate after a period of years.

4. How do I decide whether to choose a fixed or adjustable rate mortgage?

Because interest rates and mortgage options change often, your choice of a fixed or adjustable rate mortgage should depend on the interest rates and mortgage options available when you're buying, your view of the future (generally, high inflation will mean ARM rates will go up and lower inflation that they will fall), and how willing you are to take a risk. Very risk-averse people would prefer the certainty of a fixed rate mortgage, rather than take a chance that an ARM might be cheaper in the long run.

5. My spouse and I want to buy a $300,000 house. We have good incomes and can make high monthly payments, but we don't have $60,000 to make a 20% down payment. What are our other options?

Assuming you can afford (and qualify for) high monthly mortgage payments and have an excellent credit history, you should be able to find a low (10%–15%) down payment loan for a $300,000 house. However, you may have to pay a higher interest rate and loan fees than someone making a higher down payment. In addition, be prepared to purchase private mortgage insurance (PMI), which is designed to reimburse a mortgage lender up to a certain amount if you default on your loan and the foreclosure sale price is less than the amount you owe the lender (the mortgage and the costs of the sale).

6. What's the best way to find and work with a real estate agent or broker?

Get recommendations from people who have purchased a house in the past few years and whose judgment you trust. Don't work with an agent you meet at an open house or who solicits you in other ways unless and until you thoroughly check the person out. The agent or broker you choose should be in the full-time business of selling real estate and have, ideally, at least the following five traits: integrity, business sophistication, experience with the type of services you need, knowledge of the area you want to live in and sensitivity to your tastes and needs.

All states regulate and license real estate agents and brokers. While you may have different options as to the type of legal relationship you have with an agent or broker, normally, the seller pays the commission of the real estate salesperson who helps the buyer locate the seller's house. The commission is a percentage (typically 5% to 7%) of the sales price of the house. What this means is that your agent or broker has a built-in conflict of interest: Unless you've agreed to pay her separately, she won't get paid until you buy a home, and the more you pay for a house, the bigger her cut.

In short, when you evaluate the suitability of a house, it's not wise to rely principally on the advice of a person with a significant financial stake in your buying it. You need to be knowledgeable about the house-buying process, your ideal affordable house and neighborhood, your financing needs and options, your legal rights and how to evaluate comparable prices.

7. I want to buy a newly built house. Anything special I need to know?

The most important factor in buying a newly built house is not what you buy (that is, the particular model), but rather from whom you buy. Shop for an excellent builder—someone who builds quality houses, delivers on time and stands behind his or her work. To check out a particular builder, talk to existing owners in the development you're considering, or ask an experienced contractor to look at other houses the developer is building.

Many developers of new housing will help you arrange financing; some will also pay a portion of your monthly mortgage or subsidize your interest payments for a short period of time (called a "buydown" of the mortgage). As with any loan, be sure you comparison shop before arranging financing through a builder.

Also, be sure to negotiate the prices of any add-ons and upgrades. These can add substantially to the cost of a new home. And finally, check out any restrictions on how your property can be used and the responsibilities of homeowners. These are called covenants, conditions and restrictions (CC&Rs). CC&Rs commonly limit the colors you can paint your house and even the type of front yard landscaping you can do. Some developments have so many restrictions that it's almost as if your house is part of a common park, over which you have little say.

8. I'm making an offer to buy a house, but I don't want to lock myself into a deal that might not work out. How can I protect myself?

Real estate offers almost always contain contingencies—events that must happen within a certain amount of time (such as 30 to 60 days) or else the deal won't become final. For example, you may want to make your offer contingent on your qualifying for financing, the house passing certain physical inspections or even your being able to sell your existing house first. Be aware, however, that the more contingencies you place in an offer, the less likely the seller is to accept it.

9. How can I make sure I'm buying a house in good shape?

Before you finalize your house purchase, be sure to arrange inspections for defects or malfunctions in the building's structure such as the roof or windows.

In a few states (including California and Maine), you may have the advantage of a law that requires sellers to disclose considerable information about the condition of the house as well as disclose potential hazards from floods, earthquakes, fires, environmental hazards and other problems. In most states, however, houses are sold with a caveat emptor (buyer beware) approach. As long as the seller doesn't fraudulently conceal defects, the buyer is responsible for discovering the physical problems.

Regardless of whether or not the seller provides disclosures, there are certain steps most home buyers should follow, particularly if the property is old and in questionable condition. You should first conduct your own inspection. Ideally, you should do this before you make a formal written offer so that you can save yourself the trouble should you find serious problems. *How to Inspect a House* , by George Hoffman (Addison Wesley) shows how to discover major problems such as a bad foundation, leaky roof or malfunctioning fireplace.

In addition to inspecting the house yourself, hire a general contractor to inspect all major house systems, from top to bottom. Depending on the age, condition and location of the property, you may want to arrange inspections for pest damage and hazards from floods, earthquakes and other natural disasters. Professional inspections should be done after your written purchase offer has been accepted by the seller (which should be contingent upon your approving the results of one or more inspections).

If the house is in good shape, you can proceed, knowing that you're getting what you paid for. If inspections discover problems, you can negotiate with the seller to have him pay for necessary repairs, or you can back out of the deal, assuming your contract is properly written to allow you to do so.

For More Help

100 Questions Every First Time Home Buyer Should Ask, by Ilyce R. Glink (Times Books), is a substantial book designed to help first-time buyers through the maze of buying a house.

The Common-Sense Mortgage: How to Cut the Cost of Home Ownership by $100,000 or More, by Peter G. Miller (HarperPerennial), provides information to help you intelligently finance a home.

Your New House: The Alert Consumer's Guide to Buying and Building a Quality Home, by Alan & Denise Fields (Windsor Peak Press), offers advice for those who want to buy or build a new home.

How to Inspect a House, by George Hoffman (Addison Wesley), shows how to inspect a house in order to discover major problems such as a bad foundation, leaky roof or malfunctioning fireplace.

How to Buy a House in California, by Ralph Warner, Ira Serkes and George Devine (Nolo Press), explains all the details of the California house-buying process and contains tear out contracts and disclosure forms.

3. DEEDS

Remember playing Monopoly as a kid, where amassing deeds to property—those little color-coded cards—was all-important? Real-life deeds aren't nearly so colorful, but they're still very, very important. Here are some questions commonly asked about deeds.

1. What is a deed?

A deed is the document that transfers ownership of real estate. It contains the names of the old and new owners and a legal description of the property, and is signed by the person transferring the property.

2. Do I need a deed to transfer property?

Almost always. You can't transfer real estate without having something in writing. In some situations, a document other than a deed is used—for example, in a divorce, a court order may transfer real estate from the couple to just one of them.

3. I'm confused by all the different kinds of deeds—quitclaim deed, grant deed, warranty deed. Does it matter which kind of deed I use?

Probably not. Usually, what's most important is the substance of the deed: the description of the property being transferred and the names of the old and new owners. Here's a brief rundown of the most common types of deeds:

A **quitclaim deed** transfers whatever ownership interest you have in the property. It makes no guarantees about the extent of your interest. Quitclaim deeds are commonly used by divorcing couples; one spouse signs all his rights in the couple's real estate over to the other. This can be especially useful if it isn't clear how much of an interest, if any, one spouse has in property that's held in another spouse's name.

A **grant deed** transfers your ownership and implies certain promises—that the title hasn't already been transferred to someone else or been encumbered, except as set out in the deed. This is the most commonly used kind of deed, in most states.

A **warranty deed** transfers your ownership and explicitly promises the buyer that you have good title to the property. It may make other promises as well, to address particular problems with the transaction.

4. Does a deed have to be notarized?

Yes. The person who signs the deed (the person who is transferring the property) should take the deed to a notary public, who will sign and stamp it. The notarization means that a notary public has verified that the signature on the deed is genuine. The signature must be notarized before the deed will be accepted for recording (see Question 5).

5. After a deed is signed and notarized, do I have to put it on file anywhere?

Yes. You should "record" (file) the deed in the land records office in the county where the property is located. This office goes by different names in different states; it's usually called the County Recorder's Office, Land Registry Office or Register of Deeds. In most counties, you'll find it in the courthouse.

Recording a deed is simple. Just take the signed, original deed to the land records office. The clerk will take the deed, stamp it with the date and some numbers, make a copy and give the original back to you. The numbers are usually book and page numbers, which show where the deed will be found in the county's filing system. There will be a small fee, probably about $5 a page, for recording.

6. What's a trust deed?

A trust deed (also called a deed of trust) isn't like the other types of deeds; it's not used to transfer property. It's really just a version of a mortgage, commonly used in some states (California, for example).

A trust deed transfers title to land to a "trustee," usually a trust or title company, which holds the land as security for a loan. When the loan is paid off, title is transferred to the borrower. The trustee has no powers unless the borrower defaults on the loan; then the trustee can sell the property and pay the lender back from the proceeds, without first going to court.

For More Help

The Deeds Book, by Mary Randolph (Nolo Press), contains tear-out deed forms and instructions for transferring California real estate.

For information about deeds in other states, check your local law library.

4. MAKING YOUR HOME SAFE FROM BREAK-INS

Most burglars prefer to enter an empty house and get in and out quickly. Here are ten ways to avoid making your house an easy target.

1. Burglar-proof your house.

If you've been meaning to get better locks, an alarm system, metal bars on windows or motion sensor lights, do it now. Cut down shrubbery that gives burglars a hiding place. Pay special attention to back doors and windows, where burglars often find the easiest entry. See if a police department representative will evaluate your home's security and recommend improvements.

2. Lock up.

Half of all burglaries occur through unlocked doors and windows. Don't hide keys in obvious places, such as under a doormat or flowerpot, on top of the door frame or under a plant. If you have to hide a key, put it in the spot where it is least likely to be discovered.

3. Have a trusted person house-sit.

Or ask a friend, relative or neighbor to keep an eye on things. Some police departments provide security checks for vacationers.

4. Give your house a lived-in look.

An overstuffed mailbox and yellowing newspapers signal that no one is home; have someone pick up your mail and newspapers or have deliveries put on hold.

Arrange to have the lawn mowed, garden watered, leaves raked or snow shoveled. You may even want to have your neighbor put garbage in your garbage cans.

5. Fill up the driveway.

If you have two cars, leave one in the driveway, or ask a neighbor to park there.

6. Put lights on automatic timers.

Inexpensive timers turn lights and radios on and off at set times. For instance, a radio and lamp in the living room might be on in the early evening, and then a bedroom lamp could be on from 11:30 to midnight. You might also consider installing motion sensitive lights for your back yard or back entrance, or other spots where someone might hide.

7. Leave drapes and shades the way you normally have them.

If you can, have someone open drapes during the day and shut them at night. A house that's shuttered up tight looks unoccupied.

8. Put valuables out of sight.

Don't leave valuables such as jewelry, art and electronic equipment in sight, close to windows. Even simple steps to hide your property may be effective if an intruder does manage to get in. A dusty hatbox in the top of a closet, laundry hamper, empty food containers or toy box are all places to stash valuables. As an extra precaution, consider leaving some valuables with a trusted neighbor, friend or relative—if that house is secure and someone will be home the entire time you're gone.

9. Consider a safe.

If you need to protect very expensive property, consider getting a safe deposit box or buying a good fireproof safe.

10. Make a Home Inventory

If your home is struck by a burglary, an up-to-date home inventory will make it easier to deal with police and your insurance company. Without one, you'll have to create a list of all your property from memory. (An inventory is also very useful if you lose property as a result of a fire, earthquake, flood or other natural disaster.)

Fortunately, making a home inventory isn't an onerous task. And doing so not only prepares you for possible losses—it can also help you prevent the loss itself. As you inventory your possessions, you'll become more aware of their vulnerability, and you can take steps to secure them.

Start by walking through your house with a pad of paper and a still or video camera. Take pictures and jot down a list of any items worth more than $25 or $50. Go room by room, and don't forget the garage, attic and basement. Be sure to include jewelry, clothing, stamp or coin collections, CD and record collections, silver, tools and electronic equipment. Then take a little time to formalize your inventory. Insurance companies often supply inventory forms. Making and updating an inventory can be even easier if you own a computer.

Whatever your method, record key information about each item:

- Complete description, including whether or not it's marked with a serial number or an ID number such as your driver's license number. (You can buy an electric engraving pen for $20 or so at a hardware store.) ID and serial numbers will help police identify stolen goods. Also, remember to record the make and model of the item; this will help you justify its estimated value to your insurance company.
- Location. This will help you identify what you've lost if only one area, such as the garage, is hit.
- Location of ownership documents, receipts, owner's manuals and repair bills.
- Purchase price, current value and replacement cost. For most items, your best estimate will do. For antiques or other difficult-to-price items, such as a stamp collection, you may need a professional appraisal.

Keep your written and photographic inventory in a safe place, such as a fire-resistant file cabinet or safe, the freezer or a safe deposit box. Keep at least one copy away from home. If you take a long vacation, give a copy to a friend or neighbor; that way, if your house is broken into while you're gone, that person can determine what's missing and report it to the police.

For More Help

Safe Homes, Safe Neighborhoods, by Stephanie Mann with M.C. Blakeman (Nolo Press), provides detailed information on how to improve home security and reduce neighborhood crime.

Nolo's Personal RecordKeeper (Nolo Press) (software for Windows or Macintosh), allows you to create a complete home inventory on your computer.

5. Tenants' Rights

If you're a renter, there are lots of laws on the books to protect you from improper landlord conduct, including discrimination, invasion of privacy, maintaining dangerous property conditions and other landlord wrongs. Here are some of the most common questions asked by tenants about the landlord-tenant relationship. Because state laws vary—often significantly—remember to check the specific landlord-tenant statutes for your state and any local laws that may apply.

1. Why do I need to sign a lease or rental agreement?

Your lease or rental agreement is a contract. It forms the legal basis for your relationship with your landlord by setting out important issues such as:
- the length of your tenancy
- the amount of rent and deposits you must pay
- the number of people who can live on the rental property
- who pays for utilities
- whether you may have pets
- whether you may sublet the property
- the landlord's access to the rental property
- whose job it is to maintain and repair the premises, and
- who pays attorneys' fees if there is a lawsuit.

It is always wise to put your lease or rental agreement in writing, even though most states allow them to be oral (spoken). While oral agreements may seem easy and informal, if you and your landlord later disagree about key agreements, you are all too likely to end up in court, arguing over who said what to whom, when and in what context. This is particularly a problem with long-term leases, so many states prohibit oral agreements that are to last for one year or more.

2. What's the difference between a rental agreement and a lease?

The big difference is the period of occupancy. Written rental agreements provide for a tenancy for a short period (often 30 days). Your tenancy is automatically renewed at the end of this period unless you or your landlord end it by giving written notice, typically 30 days. For these month-to-month rentals (meaning the rent is paid monthly), the landlord can change terms of your agreement with proper written notice (subject to any rent control laws). This notice is usually 30 days, but can be shorter in some states if the rent is paid weekly or bi-weekly.

A written lease gives you the right to occupy a rental unit for a set term—most often for six months or a year but sometimes longer—as long as you pay the rent and comply with other lease provisions. Unlike a rental agreement, when a lease expires it does not automatically renew itself (a tenant who stays on with the landlord's consent will generally be considered a month-to-month tenant). With a fixed-term lease, the landlord cannot raise the rent or change other terms of the tenancy during the lease, unless they are specifically called for in the lease, or you agree.

3. I signed a year-long lease a few months ago, but now I want to move out. What happens if I break the lease?

As a general rule, neither you nor your landlord may properly break the lease before the term ends unless the other party significantly violates the lease. This means that you can legally move out for a good cause—for example, if your landlord fails to make necessary repairs. If you break the lease without good cause, you'll be responsible for the remainder of the rent due under the lease term. In most states, however, a landlord has a legal duty to try to find a new tenant as soon as possible—no matter what your reason for leaving—rather than charge you for the total remaining rent due under the lease.

4. I think a landlord discriminated against me when she refused to rent me an apartment. What are my rights under the law?

Under federal civil rights and fair housing laws, the landlord broke the law if she refused you the apartment because of a group characteristic such as:

- your race
- your religion
- your ethnic background or national origin
- your sex
- your age
- the fact that you have children (except in certain designated senior housing), or
- a mental or physical disability.

In addition, some state and local laws prohibit discrimination based on your marital status or sexual orientation.

On the other hand, landlords are allowed to select tenants using criteria that are based on valid business reasons, such as requiring a minimum income or a good credit rating, and applying them equally to all tenants.

5. How do I file a discrimination complaint?

If you think that a landlord has broken a federal fair housing law, contact your local office of the Department of Housing and Urban Development. To find the office nearest you, call 800-669-9777. HUD will give you a complaint form and will investigate and decide whether you have a case. You must file your complaint with HUD within one year of the alleged discriminatory act. If HUD determines that you do have a case, a mediator will try to negotiate with the landlord and reach a settlement (called a "conciliation"). If a settlement can't be reached, HUD will file a lawsuit against the landlord.

If the discrimination is a violation of a state fair housing law, you may file a complaint with the state agency in charge of enforcing the law. In California, for example, the Department of Fair Employment and Housing enforces the state's two fair housing laws. Contact your state's department of housing in order to find out whether a state housing law exists that would apply to your situation.

Also, instead of filing a complaint with HUD or a state agency, you may file a lawsuit directly in federal or state court.

6. Are there laws covering how much rent a landlord can charge, and when the rent must be paid?

Your landlord may charge any dollar amount for rent, except in certain areas covered by rent control. (States with some areas covered by rent control include California, the District of Columbia, Maryland, Massachusetts (until the end of 1996), New Jersey and New York.)

By custom, leases and rental agreements usually require rent to be paid monthly, in advance. Often rent is due on the first day of the month. However, it is usually legal for a landlord to require rent to be paid at different intervals or on a different day of the month. Unless the lease or rental agreement specifies otherwise, there is no legally-recognized grace period—in other words, if you haven't paid the rent on time, your landlord can usually start eviction proceedings the day after it is due. Some landlords charge fees for late payment of rent or for bounced checks; these fees are usually legal if they are reasonable.

For month-to-month rentals, the landlord can raise the rent (subject to any rent control laws) with proper written notice, typically 30 days. With a fixed-term lease, the landlord may not raise the rent during the lease, unless the increase is specifically called for in the lease, or you agree.

7. How much security deposit can a landlord charge?

Usually not more than a month or two worth of rent—the exact amount depends on the state in which you live. All states allow landlords to collect a security deposit when you move in; the general purpose is to assure that you pay rent when due and keep the rental unit in good condition.

Many states require landlords to put deposits in a separate account and some require landlords to pay you the interest on your deposits.

8. What are the rules for returning security deposits?

Landlords may normally make certain deductions from a tenant's security deposit, provided they do it correctly and for the right reasons. While the specific rules vary from state to state, landlords usually have a set amount of time in which to return deposits (usually 14 to 30 days after you move out—either voluntarily or by eviction). Many states require landlords to provide a written itemized accounting of deductions for unpaid rent and for repairs for damages that go beyond normal wear and tear, together with payment for any deposit balance. You may sue a landlord who fails to return your deposit when and how required, or who violates other provisions of security deposit laws such as interest requirements; often these suits may be brought in small claims court. In some states, you may recover your entire deposit—sometimes even two or three times this amount—plus attorney fees and other damages.

9. Does my landlord have the right to enter my apartment whenever he wants, without notice?

A landlord or manager may enter rented premises while you are living there without advance notice only in an emergency, such as a fire or serious water leak. Beyond that, laws in many states guarantee tenants reasonable privacy rights against landlord intrusions. Typically, a landlord has the right to legally enter rented premises in order to make needed repairs (in some states, just to assess the need for repairs) and to show the property to prospective new tenants or purchasers. Many states allow landlords the right of entry during your absence to maintain the property as necessary and to inspect for damage and needed repairs. In addition, a landlord may enter rented premises when you move out without notifying the landlord or by court order. In most cases, a landlord may not enter just to check up on you and the rental property.

States typically require landlords to provide a specific amount of notice (usually 24 or 48 hours) before entering a rental unit. In some states, such as California, landlords must provide a "reasonable" amount of notice, legally presumed to be 24 hours.

10. My apartment badly needs repairs. Isn't it the landlord's responsibility to keep things in good working order?

Landlords in all states except Alabama, Arkansas and Colorado are responsible for the physical condition of rental property, both when you move in and during your tenancy. This responsibility stems from the landlord's duty to offer and maintain housing that satisfies basic habitability requirements, such as adequate weatherproofing, available heat, water and electricity, and clean, sanitary and structurally safe premises. Even in the three states that have not adopted this habitability rule, local or state housing laws may impose substantially the same requirements on landlords.

All tenants have the responsibility to keep their own living quarters clean and sanitary. And a landlord can usually delegate his repair and maintenance tasks to the tenant in exchange for a reduction in rent. If the tenant fails to do the job, however (or does a poor job), the landlord is not excused from his responsibility to maintain habitability.

11. What are my rights if my landlord refuses to maintain the property?

If the landlord doesn't meet his legal responsibilities, you usually have several options (depending on the state), including moving out (even in the middle of a lease), paying less rent, withholding the entire rent until the problem is fixed, making necessary repairs (or hiring someone to make them and deducting the cost from next month's rent) or calling the local building inspector (who can usually order the landlord to make repairs). You can also sue the landlord for a partial refund of past rent, and in some circumstances can sue for the discomfort, annoyance and emotional distress caused by the substandard conditions. Be sure to check the laws for your state, so you know what remedies are available to you before you take action against your landlord.

12. Is my landlord liable if I'm injured on the rental property? What if a visitor is injured?

A landlord may be liable to you—or others—for injuries caused by dangerous or defective conditions on the property you rent. In order to hold the landlord responsible, however, you must be able to prove several things:

- that the landlord had control over the problem that caused the injury
- that the accident was foreseeable
- that fixing the problem would not have been unreasonably expensive or difficult, and
- that a serious injury was the probable consequence of not fixing the problem. For example, if you fall and are hurt on a broken front door step, the landlord will be liable if:
- It was the landlord's responsibility to maintain the steps (this would usually be the case, because the steps are part of the common area, which is the landlord's responsibility).
- You could prove that an accident was foreseeable (falling on a broken step is highly likely).
- You could show that the repair was relatively easy.
- You can prove that the probable result of a broken step is a serious injury (a fall certainly qualifies).

A landlord may also be liable for your injuries and property damage resulting from the criminal acts of others, but only if the criminal incident was foreseeable and the landlord could have done something to prevent it. For example, if a landlord knows (or has reason to know) about crime in the area—and especially if there have been prior criminal incidents on his property—he may be held liable if his failure to fix a defective lock or install adequate lighting facilitates a criminal assault. A landlord can also be liable for damage or injury caused by problem tenants, such as those who deal drugs.

13. What is the best way for me to resolve a dispute with my landlord?

Legal disputes—actual and potential—come in all shapes and sizes for tenants. Whether it's a disagreement over a rent increase or responsibility for repairs, rarely should lawyers and litigation be your first choice when facing a dispute with a landlord.

Here are some tips to resolve a legal dispute without immediately going to court:

1. Know your rights under federal, state and local law.
2. Make sure the terms of your lease or rental agreement are clear and unambiguous and that you understand each of them.
3. Keep copies of any correspondence and make notes of conversations with landlords about any problems—for example, if you ask your landlord to make repairs, do so in writing and keep a copy for yourself. If you have a conversation about it, write down what was said.
4. Keep communication open. If there's a problem—for example, if the landlord enters your apartment without notice—talk with the landlord to see if the issue can be resolved.
5. If you're unsuccessful at working out an agreement, but want to continue renting from the landlord, suggest mediation by a neutral, third party (often available at little or no cost from a publicly funded program).
6. If it doesn't make sense to attempt to mediate, make clear your intention to move out, sue or pursue other legal remedies.
7. ndlord in small claims court. The maximum amount you can sue for varies from state to state, but generally is less than $3,500
8. Find out whether there is a tenants' union in your area, and if so, contact that organization for advice.
9. See a lawyer. Be sure to choose someone who has experience in handling landlord-tenant matters and, if possible, is recommended by someone whose judgment you trust.

For More Help

Tenants' Rights, by Myron Moskovitz and Ralph Warner (Nolo Press), provides a detailed discussion of California landlord-tenant law.

Every Landlord's Legal Guide, by Marcia Stewart, Ralph Warner and Janet Portman (Nolo Press), is written for landlords but contains descriptions and discussions of laws—federal, state and local—pertaining to your rights as a tenant.

Everybody's Guide to Small Claims Court, by Ralph Warner (National and California Editions) (Nolo Press), can help you if you decide to bring a lawsuit against your landlord. The book explains how to evaluate your case, prepare for court and convince a judge you're right.

6. Losing or Leaving Your Job

The possibility of being fired looms large in the list of fears of most workers. While employers generally do have a free hand to hire and fire in the workplace, a number of recent laws and legal rulings restrict those rights. And many soon-to-be-former employees are surprised to find out that they have the power to negotiate some final benefits on the way out the door.

1. For what reasons can I be fired?

You can be fired for a host of traditional and obvious reasons: incompetence, excessive absences, violating certain laws or company rules, or sleeping or taking drugs on the job. And other reasons are gaining in popularity—most notably, letting employees go because of company downsizing due to a downturn in revenue, reexamination of the company's mission or a merger with another company. In most cases, an employer does not need to provide any notice before giving an employee walking papers.

Still, there are limits. Employers do not have the right to discriminate against you illegally or to violate state or federal laws, such as those controlling wages and hours. And there are a number of other more complex reasons that may make it illegal for an employer to fire you—all boiling down to the fact that an employer must deal with you fairly and honestly.

2. I've just received a warning from my employer, and I suspect I will be fired soon. What should I do?

If you find yourself on the receiving end of a disciplinary notice, there are several steps you should take to avoid losing your job.

First, be sure you understand exactly what work behavior is being challenged. If you are unclear, ask for a meeting with your supervisor or human resources staff to discuss the issue more thoroughly.

If you disagree with allegations that your work performance or behavior is poor, ask for the assessment in writing. You may want to add a written clarification to your own personnel file—but should do so only if you feel your employer's assessment is inaccurate. Take some time to reflect and perhaps discuss your situation with friends before you sit down to write. If you don't take care with your words, they could be twisted against you as evidence of your inability to work as a team player, take constructive criticism or some other convenient company slang.

Look for written company policy on discipline procedures in the employee handbook or a separate document. If the policy says certain measures "must," "will" or "shall" be followed before an employee will be dismissed, then you have more clout in demanding that the steps be followed. That may help buy you more time so that you can change your work habits, you can wait until a workplace controversy dies down or the situation improves in some other way.

Finally, read behind the lines to see whether your disciplining or firing may be discriminatory or in other ways unfair. Look particularly at the timing: Were you put on probation shortly before your rights in the company pension plan vested? Look also at uneven applications of discipline: Are women more often given substandard performance reviews or fired before being elevated to supervisor?

3. What can I do to protect any legal rights I might have before leaving my job?

Even if you decide not to challenge the legality of your firing, you will be in a much better position to enforce all of your workplace rights if you carefully document the circumstances. For example, if you apply for unemployment insurance benefits and your former employer challenges that application, you will typically need to prove that you were dismissed for reasons beyond your control.

There are a number of ways to document what happened. The most important is to keep a paper trail: record and date each work-related event such as performance reviews, commendations or reprimands, salary increases or decreases and even informal comments your supervisor makes to you about your work. Note the date, time and location for each event; which members of management were involved; and whether or not witnesses were present. Whenever possible, back up your log with materials issued by your employer, such as copies of the employee handbook, memos, brochures and employee orientation videos. In addition, ask to see your personnel file and make a copy of all reports and reviews in it.

4. I am being forced to leave my job. But before I go, my employer requires that I sign a document promising not to sue. Will this hold up in court?

An increasing number of employees who have signed waivers of their rights to file a lawsuit over their firing have later succeeded in having the courts throw out the waivers by arguing, for example, that the waivers were signed under duress. But whether signing such a waiver will prevent you from suing your former employer depends on the circumstances of your individual case—there is no way of predicting the power of a waiver in advance.

Going along with the signing will typically give you immediate severance pay. If you have doubts about the validity of your dismissal, however, withhold your signature on any waiver of your right to sue while you think over the company's offer, obtain more information and perhaps hire a lawyer. You take the chance of not getting the money and documentation that the company waves in front of you, but you will lower your risk of signing away essential rights.

5. How much severance pay am I legally entitled to get if I'm fired?

Most employers offer severance in the form of a month or two worth of salary to employees who are laid off or let go for some reason other than misconduct. But no law requires it. And whether it is given at all varies drastically from employer to employer, region to region, industry custom to industry custom.

However, an employer may be legally obligated to pay you some severance pay if you had good reason to believe you had it coming, as evidenced by:

- a written contract stating that severance will be paid
- a promise that employees would receive severance pay as documented in an employee handbook
- a history of the company paying severance to other employees in your position, or
- an oral promise that the employer would pay you severance—although you may run into difficulties proving the promise existed.

6. My biggest concern about losing my job is losing health insurance coverage. Do I have any rights?

Ironically, workers have more rights to health insurance coverage after they lose their jobs than while employed. This is because of a 1986 law, the

Consolidated Omnibus Budget Reconciliation Act (COBRA). Under COBRA, employers must offer former employees the option of continuing to be covered by the company's group health insurance plan at the workers' own expense for some time after employment ends. Family coverage is also included.

In general, COBRA gives an employee who quits or is dismissed for reasons other than gross misconduct the right to continue group health coverage for 18 months. In some other circumstances, such as the death of the employee, that employee's dependents can continue coverage for up to 36 months.

7. I just lost my job. What can I do to assure that I'll have some income until I find another job?

Act quickly. Each day that passes without money earned puts you and those who rely on you for financial support in greater risk of running into money troubles. In some states, for example, the gap between the time that a person files for unemployment insurance and the time he or she receives the first unemployment check averages six weeks. And applying for the wrong income replacement program can waste many more precious days, weeks or even months.

Here is a brief breakdown of what is covered by each of the three major income replacement programs.

- **Unemployment insurance.** This program may provide some financial help if you lose your job, temporarily or permanently, through no fault of your own.
- **Workers' compensation.** When you cannot work because of a work-related injury or illness, this is the program that is most likely to provide you with replacement income promptly. It may also pay the medical bills resulting from a workplace injury or illness; compensate you for a permanent injury, such as the loss of a limb; and provide death benefits to the survivors of workers who die from a workplace injury or illness.
- **Social Security disability insurance.** This is intended to provide income to adults who, because of injury or illness, cannot work for at least 12 months. Unlike the workers' compensation program, it does not require that your disability be caused by a workplace injury or illness.

Also consider possible income from a private disability insurance program if you were paying for it through payroll withholdings, or if your employer paid for such premiums.

In addition, a few states—including California, Hawaii, New Jersey, New York and Rhode Island—offer disability benefits as part of their unemployment insurance programs. Typical program requirements mandate that you submit your medical records and show that you requested a leave of absence from your employer. Some may also require proof that you intend to return to your job when you recover. Call the local unemployment insurance and workers' compensation insurance offices to determine whether your state is one that maintains this kind of coverage.

For More Help

Your Rights in the Workplace, by Barbara Kate Repa (Nolo Press), is a comprehensive guide to your rights as an employee.

7. WORKPLACE RIGHTS

During the early 1990s, a number of laws were passed to increase workers' rights. And other laws that have been on the books for a while—such as those guaranteeing fair pay and prohibiting discrimination against older workers—have taken on added importance while the economy is strapped. These workplace rights may help you if you have trouble on the job, but first you must be vigilant in learning about the laws and how they work.

1. I suspect my employer is bending some of the rules on paying for overtime. What are the legal controls on this?

The most important and most far-reaching law guaranteeing a worker's right to be paid fairly is the federal Fair Labor Standards Act or FLSA. The FLSA:
- defines the 40-hour workweek
- covers the federal minimum wage
- sets requirements for overtime, and
- places restrictions on child labor.

The FLSA is the single law most often violated by employers. But an employer must also comply with other local, state or federal workplace laws that set higher standards. So in addition to determining whether you are being paid properly for overtime under the FLSA, you may need to check other laws that apply to your situation. A good place to begin is to contact the local office of your state department of labor.

2. Am I entitled to take time off from work if I get sick?

The Family and Medical Leave Act (FMLA), a federal law passed in 1993, gives workers some rights to time off for medical reasons. Under the FMLA, you may be eligible for up to 12 weeks of unpaid sick leave during any 12-month period. Your employer can count your accrued paid benefits—vacation, sick leave and personal leave days—toward the 12 weeks of leave allowed under the law. But many employers give employees the option of deciding whether or not to include paid leave time as part of their 12 weeks of family leave.

The FMLA applies to all private and public employers with 50 or more employees—an estimated one-half of the workforce. To be covered under the law, you must have:
- been employed at the same workplace for a year or more, and
- worked at least 1,250 hours (about 24 hours a week) during the year preceding the leave.

There are a number of loopholes in the FMLA. Companies with fewer than 50 employees working at offices within a 75-mile radius are exempt from the FMLA—this means that small regional companies of even the largest corporations may not need to comply with the Act. The law also allows companies to exempt the highest paid 10% of employees. And finally, schoolteachers and instructors who work for educational agencies and private elementary or secondary schools may have restrictions on their FMLA leave.

3. What if a member of my family gets sick—can I take time off to care for him or her?

Possibly. The rights given to workers by the FMLA also apply if a member of your close family gets sick, or if you give birth to or adopt a child.

4. My employer refused to grant me the time off guaranteed by the FMLA. What can I do?

The FMLA is enforced by the U.S. Department of Labor. If you have specific questions about this emerging law, including how to file a claim against your employer for failing to comply, contact your local Department of Labor office. You should be able to find a listing under U.S. Government, Department of Labor, in the telephone book.

You generally must file a claim under the FMLA within two years after an employer violates the Act. If the employer's violation was willful, you'll have up to three years to file. Because the law is new and considered fairly radical, much concerning its practicality and effect—including what constitutes a willful violation by an employer—will be decided in the years to come.

5. What laws protect disabled workers from workplace discrimination?

The Americans With Disabilities Act (ADA) prohibits employment discrimination on the basis of workers' disabilities. Generally, the ADA prohibits employers from:

- discriminating on the basis of virtually any physical or mental disability
- asking job applicants questions about their past or current medical conditions
- requiring job applicants to take medical exams, and
- creating or maintaining worksites that include substantial physical barriers to the movement of people with physical disabilities.

The ADA covers companies with 15 or more employees. Its coverage broadly extends to private employers, employment agencies and labor organizations. A precursor of the ADA, the Vocational Rehabilitation Act, prohibits discrimination against disabled workers in state and federal government.

In addition, many state laws protect against discrimination based on physical or mental disability.

6. Who, exactly, does the ADA protect?

The ADA's protections extend to disabled workers—defined as people who:

- have a physical or mental impairment that substantially limits a major life activity
- have a record of impairment, or
- are regarded as having an impairment.

An impairment includes physical disorders, such as cosmetic disfigurement or loss of a limb, as well as mental and psychological disorders.

The ADA protects job applicants and employees who, although disabled as defined above, are still qualified for a particular job. In other words, they would be able to perform the essential functions of a job with some form of accommodation, such as a voice-activated computer or customized workspace. Whether a disabled worker is deemed qualified for a given job seems to depend on whether he or she has appropriate skill, experience, training or education for the position.

7. How can I take action under the ADA if I feel an employer has discriminated against me as a disabled person?

The ADA is enforced by the Equal Employment Opportunity Commission (EEOC). To start an investigation of your claim, file a complaint at the local EEOC office. Call 800-669-3362 to find the office nearest you.

If you live in a state with laws that protect workers against discrimination based on physical or mental disability, you can choose to file a complaint under your state's law, the ADA or both.

For additional information on the ADA, contact:
Office on the Americans with Disabilities Act
Civil Rights Division
U.S. Department of Justice
P.O. Box 66118
Washington, DC 20035-6118
202-514-0301 (voice) or 202-514-0381 (TDD).

8. Do I have any legal rights if I feel that my workplace is unsafe or unhealthy?

The main federal law covering threats to workplace safety is the Occupational Safety and Health Act of 1970 (OSHA). OSHA requires employers to provide a workplace that is free of dangers that could physically harm employees.

The law quite simply requires that your employer protect you from "recognized hazards" in the workplace. It does not specify or limit the types of dangers covered—it includes everything from the cause of a serious cut or bruise to the unhealthy effects of long-term exposure to some types of radiation.

Basically, to prove an OSHA violation, you must produce evidence that:
* your employer failed to keep the workplace free of a hazard, and
* the particular hazard was recognized as being likely to cause death or serious physical injury.

If you feel that your workplace is unsafe, your first action should be to make your supervisor aware of the danger. Then, if you have not been successful in getting your company to correct the safety hazard, you can file a complaint at the nearest OSHA office. Look under the U.S. Labor Department in the federal government section of your local telephone directory.

9. Does OSHA protect against the harmful effects of tobacco smoke in the workplace?

OSHA rules apply to tobacco smoke only in the most rare and extreme circumstances, such as when contaminants created by a manufacturing process combine with tobacco smoke to create a dangerous workplace air supply that fails OSHA standards. Workplace air quality standards and measurement techniques are so technical that typically only OSHA agents or consultants who specialize in environmental testing are able to determine when the air quality falls below allowable limits.

10. If OSHA won't protect me from tobacco smoke at work, what can I do?

If your health problems are severely aggravated by co-workers' smoking, there are a number of steps you can take.
* **Ask your employer for an accommodation.** Successful accommodations to smoke-sensitive workers have included installing additional ventilation systems, restricting smoking areas to outside or special rooms and segregating smokers and nonsmokers.
* **Check local and state laws.** A growing number of local and state laws prohibit smoking in the workplace. Most of them also set out specific procedures for pursuing complaints. If you can't find local laws that prohibit smoking in workplaces, check with a national nonsmokers' rights group.
* **Consider filing a federal complaint.** Most claims for injuries caused by secondhand smoke in the workplace are pressed and processed under the Americans With Disabilities Act. In the strongest complaints, workers proved that smoke sensitivity rendered them disabled in that they were unable to perform a major life activity: breathing freely.

23

- **Consider income replacement programs.** If you are unable to work out a plan to resolve a serious problem with workplace smoke, you may be forced to leave the workplace. But you may qualify for workers' compensation or unemployment insurance benefits.

11. Are there any restrictions on the kind of information my employer can keep on me?

The federal Privacy Act limits the type of information that federal agencies, the military and other government employers may keep on their workers.

Private employers, however, have a nearly unfettered hand when it comes to the kind of information they can collect. The laws in only a few states restrict the information in personnel files. Michigan, for example, bars employers from keeping records describing an employee's political associations. And in Maryland, an employer may not ask a job applicant about psychiatric or psychological illness or treatment unless it is directly related to his or her fitness to perform a job.

While many states have some type of law regulating personnel files for private employers, most of these laws control not the content of the files, but:

- whether and how employees and former employees can get access to their personnel files
- whether employees are entitled to copies of information in them, and
- how employees can correct erroneous information in the file.

12. My employer has just "downsized," giving notice to nearly one-fourth of the workforce. Most of us are older workers who have been here a while, and I suspect this is simply an attempt to save on costly benefits and higher salaries. Is there any legal protection for us?

Possibly. The federal Age Discrimination in Employment Act (ADEA) provides that workers over the age of 40 cannot be arbitrarily discriminated against because of age in any employment decision. Perhaps the single most important rule under the ADEA is that no worker can be forced to retire.

Under the ADEA, there has to be a valid reason—not related to age—for all employment decisions, especially firing. Examples of valid reasons would be poor job performance or your employer's economic troubles.

In addition, another federal law, the Older Workers Benefit Protection Act, makes it clearly illegal:

- to use an employee's age as the basis for discrimination in benefits, and
- to target older workers for staff cutting programs.

Both laws are enforced, along with other discrimination complaints, by the Equal Employment Opportunity Commission (EEOC). Call 800-669-3362 to find the EEOC office nearest you.

For More Help

Your Rights in the Workplace, by Barbara Kate Repa (Nolo Press), is a comprehensive guide to your rights as an employee.

The United States Department of Labor, 200 Constitution Avenue, NW, Washington, DC 20210, 202-219-6666, offers pamphlets describing federal wage and hours laws and the Family Medical Leave Act.

The Equal Employment Opportunity Commission, 1801 L Street, NW, Washington, DC 20507, 800-669-3362, offers pamphlets about discrimination in the workplace.

The Occupational Safety and Health Administration, 200 Constitution Avenue, NW, Washington, DC 20210, 202-219-8149, publishes pamphlets about workplace safety laws.

8. SEXUAL HARASSMENT

ON THE JOB

Sexual harassment on the job took a dramatic leap into public awareness in October 1991, when Professor Anita Hill's charges against Judge Clarence Thomas became known after his nomination to the U.S. Supreme Court. Other incidents have erupted since then, including investigations into the Navy after the Tailhook incident and into government officials after Senator Bob Packwood was accused of harassing several female staffers.

Enforcement of the laws prohibiting sexual harassment has been stepped up in the last few years. But in workplaces across America, the issue is far from settled. Sexual harassment is still a daily problem for many workers, especially women.

1. What is sexual harassment?

In legal terms, sexual harassment is any unwelcome sexual advance or conduct on the job that creates an intimidating, hostile or offensive working environment. In real life, sexually harassing behavior ranges from repeated offensive or belittling jokes to outright sexual assault.

2. Are there laws that protect against sexual harassment on the job?

Yes. But surprisingly, those laws are fairly new. In fact, prior to the 1980s, there were no federal or state laws prohibiting sexual harassment on the job and few instances in which it was prevented or punished.

The history is interesting even to those who aren't history buffs. In 1980, the Equal Employment Opportunity Commission (EEOC) issued regulations defining sexual harassment and stating it was a form of sexual discrimination prohibited by the Civil Rights Act, which had been originally passed in 1964. In 1986, the U.S. Supreme Court first ruled that sexual harassment was a form of job discrimination—and held it to be illegal.

Today, there is greater understanding that the Civil Rights Act prohibits sexual harassment at work. In addition, most states have their own fair employment practices laws that prohibit harassment—many of them more strict than the federal law. To find out the law in your state, call 800-669-3362 and ask for the EEOC office nearest you.

3. Are men ever sexually harassed? Can workers harass co-workers of the same gender?

The laws prohibiting sexual harassment on the job protect all workers. Men can—and do—sexually harass other men. Women can—and do—sexually harass men and sometimes other women.

But in the overwhelming majority of cases of sexual harassment, it's a male co-worker or supervisor who is harassing a female worker. No one is sure why this is so. Socialization probably plays a part: men are more likely than women to find sexual advances flattering, women more likely to be perceived as the gatekeepers of conduct. Economics enter, too. There are simply more women in the workforce than ever before—and at least some male workers feel the influx as a threat to their own livelihoods. Finally, sexual harassment is a power ploy, a way to keep some workers in lower-paid, less respected positions—or force them out of the workplace altogether.

4. Some workers, particularly men, are now worried that anything they say or do at work may be misinterpreted as sexual harassment. Any guidance?

The super-cautious advice—don't say anything to co-workers at work except name, rank and serial number—is surely overkill. The better approach is to use common sense. There is plenty of room to be friendly and personable without behaving in a way that is likely to offend workers of either gender.

Some rough guides for evaluating your own workplace behavior:

- Would you say or do it in front of your spouse or parents?
- Would you say or do it in front of a colleague of the same gender?
- How would you feel if your mother, wife, sister or daughter were subjected to the same words or behavior?
- How would you feel if another man said or did the same things to you?
- Does it need to be said or done at all?

If you are truly concerned that your words or conduct may be offensive to a co-worker, there is one surefire way to find out: ask.

5. I feel that I'm being sexually harassed at work. What should I do?

Keep in mind that sexual harassment is unwanted behavior. Tell the harasser to stop. Surprisingly often—some experts say up to 90% of the time—this works.

When confronted directly, harassment is especially likely to end if it is at a fairly low level: off-color jokes, inappropriate comments about your appearance, repeated requests for dates, tacky cartoons tacked onto the office refrigerator.

Saying "no" in a tangible way does more than assert your determination to stop the behavior. It is also a crucial first step if you later decide to take more formal action against the harasser, whether through your company's complaint procedure or through the legal system. And give serious thought to documenting what's going on; your case will be stronger if you can later prove that the harassment continued after you confronted the harasser.

6. But confronting a harasser sounds scary. What's the best way to do it?

If possible, deal directly with the harassment when it occurs. But if your harasser surprises you with an obnoxious gesture or comment that catches you completely off-guard—a common tactic—you may be too flabbergasted to respond at once. Or if you did respond, you may not have expressed yourself clearly. Either way, talk to him or her the next day.

Keep the conversation brief. Try to speak to your harasser privately—out of the hearing range of supervisors and co-workers. Do not smile, touch your harasser or give any other mixed messages when you speak. And this is not a good time to use humor to make your point. Finally, it is usually better to make a direct request that a specific kind of behavior stop, rather than to describe to your harasser how you feel.

If your harasser persists, write a letter, spelling out what behavior you object to and why. Also, specify what you want to happen next. If you feel the situation is serious or bound to escalate, let him or her know that you will take action against the harassment if it doesn't stop at once. If your company has a written policy against harassment, you may want to attach a copy of it to your letter.

7. What if the harassment doesn't stop even after I've confronted the harasser?

It is impossible to offer foolproof advice on how to respond to every situation involving serious sexual harassment. But it's usually best to get official help either from your employer or a state or federal agency. Prepare to do this by collecting as much detailed evidence as possible about the specifics of your harassment.

Be sure to save any offensive letters, photographs, cards or notes you receive. And if you were made to feel uncomfortable because of jokes, pin-ups or cartoons posted at work, confiscate them—or at least make copies. An anonymous, obnoxious photo or joke posted on a bulletin board is not anyone else's personal property, so you are free to take it down and keep it as evidence. If that's not possible, photograph the workplace walls. Note the dates the offensive material was posted—and whether there were hostile reactions when you took it down or asked another person to do so.

Also, keep a detailed journal. Write down the specifics of everything that feels like harassment. Include the names of everyone involved, what happened, where and when it took place. If anyone else saw or heard the harassment, note that as well. Be as specific as possible about what was said and done—and how it affected you, your health or job performance.

If your employer has conducted periodic evaluations of your work, make sure you have copies. In fact, you may want to ask for a copy of your entire personnel file—before you tip your hand that you are considering taking action against a harassing co-worker. Your records will be particularly persuasive evidence if your evaluations have been good and your employer later retaliates by trying to transfer or fire you, claiming poor job performance.

8. If the harassment still doesn't stop, what are my options short of filing a lawsuit or a complaint with a government agency?

If you have already sent your harasser a letter demanding that the behavior stop, you may want to take more forceful action. Consider giving a copy of your letter to his or her supervisor—along with a memo explaining that the behavior has become more outrageous.

If the harassment still does not abate, send the letter to the next-ranked worker or official at your workplace. Include a cover letter in which you offer your own remedy for the situation—something realistic that might help end the discomfort, such as transferring the harasser to a more distant worksite. If it's your own supervisor who has been harassing you, consider asking to be assigned a different supervisor.

These days, most workplaces have specific written policies prohibiting sexual harassment. If you have followed the steps that seem reasonable to you but the harassment continues, your next option is to pursue any procedure your company has established for handling harassment.

9. What legal steps can I take to end the harassment?

If all investigation and settlement attempts fail to produce satisfactory results, your next step may be to file a lawsuit for damages under the federal Civil Rights Act or under a state fair employment practices statute.

Even if you intend right from the beginning to file such a lawsuit, you sometimes must first file a claim with a government agency. For example, an employee pursuing a claim under the Civil Rights Act must first file a claim with the EEOC, and a similar procedure is required under some state laws. The EEOC or state agency may decide to prosecute your case on its own, but that happens only occasionally.

More commonly, at some point, the agency will issue you a document referred to as a "right-to-sue" letter that allows you to take your case to court. When filing an action for sexual harassment, you will almost always need to hire a lawyer for help.

For More Help

Sexual Harassment on the Job, by William Petrocelli and Barbara Kate Repa (Nolo Press), explains what sexual harassment is and how to stop it.

9. Repaying Debts and Dealing With Creditors

If you're in debt, you probably feel very alone. But you shouldn't. All over the country, disposable incomes are down, savings are evaporating, big businesses are merging (and laying people off), the military is downsizing—and people are just generally struggling to get by. Here are some specific suggestions for dealing with debts—and creditors.

1. I feel completely overwhelmed by my debts and don't know where to begin. What should I do?

Take a deep breath and realize that for the most part, your creditors want to help you. Whether you're behind on your bills or are afraid of getting behind, call your creditors. Let them know what's going on—job loss, reduction in hours, medical problem, big tax bill or whatever—and ask for help. Suggest possible solutions such as a temporary reduction of your payments, skipping a few payments and tacking them on at the end of a loan, skipping a few payments and paying them off over a few months, dropping late fees and other charges or even rewriting a loan. If you need help negotiating with your creditors, consider contacting a local Consumer Credit Counseling Service office.

2. I'm afraid I might miss a car payment—should I just let the lender repossess?

No. Before your car payment is due, call the lender and ask for some time. If you're at least a few months into the loan and haven't missed any payments, the lender will probably let you miss one or two months payments and tack them on at the end. If you don't pay or contact the lender, the lender can repossess the car one minute after midnight the day after the payment was due. The lender doesn't have to warn you, although many will as a courtesy. If your car is repossessed, you'll have a chance to get it back by paying the entire balance due and the cost of repossession or, in some cases, by paying the cost of the repossession and the missed payments, and then making payments under your contract. If you don't get the car back, the lender will sell it at an auction for far less than it's worth. You'll still owe the lender the difference between the balance of your loan and what the sale brings in. The amount is usually in the thousands.

3. What if I can't make the payments on my car lease?

First, review your lease agreement. If your total obligation is under $25,000 and the term exceeds four months (virtually all car leases meet these requirements), your lease agreement must disclose the following:

- A written statement of costs, including the amount of any advance payment, the number and amount of regular payments and the amount of any license, registration, taxes and maintenance fees.
- Other terms of the lease, such as insurance requirements and extended warranties to which you are entitled.

- Whether you are obligated to pay only the monthly payments (closed-ended lease), or whether you'll have a balloon payment at the end (open-ended lease).

If any required terms were not disclosed, you have a right to terminate the lease without paying any penalty.

To cancel your lease, look at the early termination provision. You may simply owe a small amount of money if you cancel. If you'll owe a ridiculous sum or you can't figure out the amount because the formula is too complex to understand, you can assert your right to cancel on the ground that the formula is unreasonable or wasn't properly disclosed to you.

If you terminate your lease early and still owe a large balance, you can try to negotiate with the lease company to pay a reduced amount or to extend your payments over time.

4. How soon after I miss a house payment will the bank begin foreclosure proceedings?

This varies from state to state and lender to lender, but most lenders don't start formal foreclosure proceedings until you've missed four or five payments. Before taking back your house, a lender would rather rewrite the loan, suspend principal payments for while (have you pay interest only), reduce your payments or even allow you to miss a few payments and spread them out over time.

5. My credit card debt is consuming my life. How can I cut credit card costs?

If you have more than one card, pay down the balances with the highest interest rates and then use (or obtain) a card with a low rate. Because credit card companies want to remain competitive, you might get a rate reduction simply by calling your current company and asking. You may also be able to get your credit card company to do away with annual fees. Understand that paying with credit cards (and carrying a balance on those cards) is a poor way to manage your money. The average credit card interest rate is still 17%; you might be able to get a bank loan at a much lower rate to make substantial purchases.

6. I owe a lot of money to the IRS. What can I do?

If you haven't been in trouble with the IRS in the past and you owe under $10,000, the IRS will grant you an installment plan to pay off your taxes. If your bill is so high there is no way you'll ever be able to pay it off, you may be able to reduce it through an IRS program called an "offer in compromise." This means you offer to pay the IRS an amount you can afford in one lump sum. The amount must be at least the value of your non-necessary property. If the IRS accepts your offer, your balance is wiped out. Finally, you may be able to use bankruptcy to eliminate, reduce, or spread out your IRS payments.

7. My utility bill was huge because of a very cold winter. Do I have to pay it all at once?

Probably not. Most utility companies offer customers an amortization program. This means that if your bills are higher in certain months than others, the company averages your yearly bills so you can spread out the large bills. Also, if you are elderly, disabled or low-income, you may be eligible for reduced rates—ask your utility company.

8. I'm swamped with student loans and can't afford my payments. What can I do to avoid default?

First, know that you're right to do all you can to avoid default, rather than ignoring your loans and hoping they'll just go away. Since the statute of limitations for collecting student loans was eliminated in 1991, there's no way to run from your loans—the government may find you and begin collections at any time. And if you've defaulted, the amount you owe will probably have skyrocketed, because the government can add a collections fee of up to 43%. It's far better to face your lenders and try to work out a payment plan you can live with.

Contact your lenders or the companies who service your student loans and let them know why you're having trouble making your payments. You may be eligible for a deferment or forbearance—ways of postponing repayment. In very limited circumstances, you may even be allowed to cancel a loan. Also, talk to your lenders about flexible payment options—many are now offering payments geared to borrowers' incomes. You can also try to negotiate with your lender as you would with any other creditor—your lender may be willing to reduce your payments or extend your overall time to make payments.

You may also want to consider consolidating your student loans. You can consolidate federal student loans through the government's direct lending program or through a private loan servicing company, such as Sallie Mae or USA Group. With loan consolidation, you can lower your monthly payments by extending your repayment period; you may also be able to lower your interest rate. Most loan consolidators offer flexible repayment options based on your income, and you can probably consolidate even if one or more of your loans is in default. Types of loans eligible for consolidation, repayment options and interest rates vary slightly from lender to lender. Contact loan servicers for more information:

- Federal Direct Consolidation Loan Center: 800-455-5889
- Sallie Mae: 800-524-9100
- USA Group: 800-382-4506.

9. I defaulted on a student loan a long time ago and now they want me to pay. I can't afford very much, but I can pay something. Any suggestions?

The Higher Education Amendments of 1992 require that the holder of a student loan accept "reasonable and affordable" payments, based on your income and expenses. The holder cannot insist on a monthly minimum, although many demand at least $50. If you make 12 consecutive reasonable and affordable payments, the lender must remove the default notice from your credit record.

10. I paid off my student loan a long time ago, but the Department of Education recently wrote me saying I still owe it. Help!

You need to get documentation. First, contact your school and ask for a report from the Department of Education showing the loan's status. Then, think about ways you can show that you paid the loan: Do you have canceled checks or old bank statements? Can you get microfiche or other electronic copies of checks from your bank or the government regulatory agency if your bank is out of business? Does a former roommate or spouse remember seeing you write a check every month? Can you get old credit reports (check with lenders from whom you've borrowed in years past) which may show a payment status on an old loan? Get old tax returns (from the IRS, if necessary), showing that you itemized the interest deduction on student loan payments back when that was permitted. Any of these things will help you prove to the Department of Education that you paid your loan.

11. When can a creditor garnish my wages, place a lien on my house, seize my bank account or take my tax refund?

For the most part, a creditor must sue you, obtain a court judgment and then solicit the help of a sheriff or other law enforcement official to garnish wages. Even then, the maximum the creditor can take is 25% of your net pay—and you can challenge that in court if you can't live on only 75% of your wages. Three creditors can garnish wages without first suing: The IRS can take everything but about $100 a week, the Department of Education can garnish up to 10% of your wages if you're in default, and up to 50% of your wages can be garnished to pay a child support or alimony debt.

To place a lien on your house or empty your bank account, almost all creditors must first sue you, get a judgment and then use a law enforcement officer. A few creditors, such as an unpaid contractor who worked on your house, can put a lien on your house without suing. And again, the IRS is an exception—it can place a lien or empty your bank account without suing first.

Your tax refund can never be taken unless the Treasury Department receives such a request from the IRS, the Department of Education or a child support collection agency.

12. Can I go to jail for not paying my debts?

Debtor's prisons were eliminated in the U.S. around 1900. In a few unusual situations, however, you could be jailed: you willfully violate a court order, especially an order to pay child support; you are convicted of willfully refusing to pay income taxes; or you are about to conceal yourself or your property to avoid paying a debt for which a creditor has a judgment against you (this is extremely rare).

For More Help

Money Troubles: Legal Strategies to Cope With Your Debts, by Robin Leonard (Nolo Press), explains your legal rights and offers practical strategies for dealing with debts and creditors.

Stand Up to the IRS, by Frederick W. Daily (Nolo Press), provides information and strategies for handling tax debts.

How to Get Out of Debt, Stay Out of Debt, & Live Prosperously, by Jerrold Mundis (Bantam) explains how to live—happily—without credit.

The Federal Trade Commission, 6th & Pennsylvania Ave., NW, Washington, DC 20850, 202-326-2222, publishes free pamphlets on debts and credit, including *Building a Better Credit Record, Buying and Borrowing: Cash in on the Facts, Cosigning a Loan, Credit and Older Americans, Credit Billing Errors, Credit Practices Rule, Equal Credit Opportunity, Fair Credit Billing, Fair Credit Reporting, Fix Your Own Credit Problems and Save Money, Getting a Loan: Your Home as Security, Lost or Stolen Credit and ATM Cards, Solving Credit Problems* and *Women and Credit Histories.*

The Federal Deposit Insurance Corporation, 550 17th St., NW, Washington, DC 20429, 202-393-8400, publishes free pamphlets about credit, including *Equal Credit Opportunity and Age, Fair Credit Billing, Fair Credit Reporting Act* and *How the Equal Credit Opportunity Act Affects You.*

The Federal Student Aid Information Center, P.O. Box 84, Washington, DC 20044, 800-433-3243, provides information about federal student loan programs.

10. Debt Collections

The law prohibits debt collectors from using abusive or deceptive tactics to collect a debt. But the law gives creditors and debt collectors powerful collection tools once they have won a lawsuit for the debt. Here are eight frequently asked questions and answers about debt collections.

1. Collection agencies have been calling me all hours of the day and night. How can I get them to stop contacting me?

It's against the law for a bill collector who works for a collection agency (as opposed to working in the collections department of the creditor itself) to call you before 8 am or after 9 pm. The law, the Fair Debt Collection Practices Act (FDCPA), also bars collectors from calling you at work, harassing you, using abusive language, making false or misleading statements, adding unauthorized charges and many other practices. Under the FDCPA, you have the right to demand that the collection agency stop contacting you, except to tell you that collection efforts have ended or that the creditor or collection agency will sue you. You must put your request in writing.

2. I'm also getting calls and letters from the collections department of a local merchant I did business with. Can I tell that collector to stop contacting me?

No. The FDCPA applies only to bill collectors who work for collection agencies. Several states, including California, Florida, Hawaii, Louisiana, Maryland, Massachusetts, Michigan, Oregon, Texas and Wisconsin, have laws which bar all debt collectors—both working for a collection agency and working for the creditor itself—from harassing, abusing, or threatening you, or making any false or misleading statement. These state laws, however, don't give you the right to demand that the collector stop contacting you. There is one exception: Residents of New York City can use a local consumer protection law to write any bill collector and say "Stop!"

3. I just got a form collection letter with a lawyer's mechanically reproduced signature on it. Is this a legitimate collection technique?

Perhaps not. Under the FDCPA, a lawyer must review each individual collection case before putting his or her name on a collection letter. The lawyer can't simply authorize that a form letter be sent and then let the bill collector send it, with the lawyer's signature, if the lawyer hasn't reviewed the particular debtor's file.

If you get such a letter, the lawyer may be violating the FDCPA. You probably have a basis to sue the lawyer and collection agency—even in small claims court.

4. A bill collector insisted that I wire the money I owe through Western Union. Am I required to do so?

No, and it could add a lot to your debt if you did. Many collectors, especially when a debt is more than 90-days past due, will suggest several "urgency payment" options, including:

- Sending money by express or overnight mail. This will add at least $10 to your bill—a first class stamp is fine.
- Wiring money through Western Union's Quick Collect or American Express' Moneygram—another $10 waste.
- Putting your payment on a credit card not charged to its maximum. You'll never get out of debt if you do this.

5. I've moved a lot and recently heard from a collector on a bill that's almost three years old. How did the collector find me?

In this technological age, it's easy to run but harder to hide. Collectors use many different resources to find debtors. They may contact relatives, friends, neighbors and employers, posing as long-lost friends to get these people to reveal your new whereabouts. In addition, collectors often get information from post office change of address forms, state motor vehicle registration information, voter registration records, former landlords and banks.

6. Can a collection agency add interest to my debt?

Not unless your original agreement calls for the addition of interest during collection proceedings, or the addition of such interest is allowed under your state's law. Many states do authorize the collection of such interest. In California, for example, collection agencies can add interest because the Civil Code permits a creditor to charge interest after default, even if the contract doesn't say anything about interest.

7. A collection agency sued me and won. Will I still be called and sent letters demanding payment?

No. Before obtaining a court judgment, a bill collector generally has only one way of getting paid: ask for (or demand) payment. This is done with calls and letters. You can ignore the phone calls and throw out your mail, and the collector can't do much else. (Though if your debt is secured—meaning you pledged property as security for payment of the debt—the collector may be able to grab the security.) Once the collector (or creditor) has a judgment, however, you can expect more aggressive collections actions. If you have a job, the collector will try to garnish up to 25% of your net wages. The collector may also try to levy on any bank, credit union or money market account. If you own real property, the collector will probably record a lien, which will hurt your credit rating. Even if you're not currently working or have no property, you're not home free.

Depending on the state, court judgments can last up to 20 years—and in many states, can be renewed.

8. What can I do if a bill collector violates the FDCPA?

First, try to get someone to witness the violation. You can "invite" the collector back to your home or call the collector back on the phone and repeat whatever you said the first time that caused the collector to make the illegal statement(s). Then file a complaint. You can even file a complaint if you don't have a witness, but a witness helps.

File your first complaint with the Federal Trade Commission (address and phone number are at the end of this section). Next, complain to your state consumer protection agency. Finally, send a copy of your complaint to the creditor who hired the collection agency. If the violations are severe enough, the creditor may stop the collection efforts.

If the violations are ongoing or outrageous, you can sue a collection agency for up to $1,000 in small claims court for violating the FDCPA. You probably won't win if you can prove only a few minor violations.

For More Help

Money Troubles: Legal Strategies to Cope With Your Debts, by Robin Leonard (Nolo Press), explains your legal rights and offers practical strategies for dealing with debts and creditors.

The Federal Trade Commission, 6th & Pennsylvania Ave., NW, Washington, DC 20850, 202-326-2222, publishes free pamphlets on debts and credit, including *Building a Better Credit Record, Buying and Borrowing: Cash in on the Facts, Cosigning a Loan, Credit and Older Americans, Credit Billing Errors, Credit Practices Rule, Equal Credit Opportunity, Fair Credit Billing, Fair Credit Reporting, Fix Your Own Credit Problems and Save Money, Getting a Loan: Your Home as Security, Lost or Stolen Credit and ATM Cards, Solving Credit Problems* and *Women and Credit Histories.*

The Federal Deposit Insurance Corporation, 550 17th St., NW, Washington, DC 20429, 202-393-8400, publishes free pamphlets about credit, including *Equal Credit Opportunity and Age, Fair Credit Billing, Fair Credit Reporting Act* and *How the Equal Credit Opportunity Act Affects You.*

11. BANKRUPTCY

If you are seriously in debt, you might consider filing for bankruptcy. Here are some common questions designed to help you understand the bankruptcy process and what bankruptcy can and cannot do for you.

1. What exactly is bankruptcy?

Bankruptcy is a federal court procedure created to help consumers and businesses eliminate their debts or repay them while under the protection of the bankruptcy court. Congress passed the first American bankruptcy law around 1800, modeled on the English bankruptcy system. Bankruptcy's roots can be traced to the Bible. (Deuteronomy 15:1-2—"Every seventh year you shall practice remission of debts. This shall be the nature of the remission: Every creditor shall remit the due that he claims from his neighbor; he shall not dun his neighbor or kinsman.")

2. Aren't there different kinds of bankruptcy?

Yes. Bankruptcies can generally be described as "liquidation" or "reorganization" bankruptcies.

Liquidation bankruptcy is called Chapter 7. Under Chapter 7, a consumer or a business asks the bankruptcy court to wipe out (discharge) the debts owed. Certain types of debts cannot be discharged in Chapter 7—these are discussed in Question 5. In exchange for the discharge of debts, the business' assets or the consumer's nonexempt property is sold—that is, liquidated—and the proceeds are used to pay off creditors. Consumers rarely lose property in Chapter 7 bankruptcy.

There are several types of reorganization bankruptcy. Consumers with debts in excess of $1 million or businesses can file for Chapter 11—a complex, time consuming and expensive process. Family farmers can file for Chapter 12. And Chapter 13 is for consumers with debts under $1 million. In a reorganization bankruptcy, you file a plan with the bankruptcy court, proposing how you will repay your creditors. Some debts must be repaid in full; others you pay only a percentage; others aren't paid at all. Some debts you have to pay with interest; some are paid at the beginning of your plan and some at the end.

3. What generally happens in consumer bankruptcy cases?

In a Chapter 7 case, you file several forms with the bankruptcy court listing income and expenses, assets, debts and property transactions for the past two years. The cost to file is $160, which may be waived for people who receive public assistance or live below the poverty level. A court-appointed person, the trustee, is assigned to oversee your case. About a month after filing, you must attend a "meeting of creditors" where the trustee goes over your forms and asks any questions. Despite the name, creditors rarely attend. If you have any nonexempt property, you must give it (or its value in cash) to the trustee. The meeting lasts about five minutes. Three to six months later, you receive a notice from the court that "all debts that qualified for discharge were discharged." Then your case is over.

Chapter 13 is a little different. You file the same forms, plus a proposed repayment plan, in which you describe how you intend to repay your debts over the next three, or in some cases five, years. The cost to file is $160 (it cannot be waived) and a trustee is assigned to oversee the case. Here, too, you attend the meeting of creditors, but often one or two creditors attend this meeting, especially if they don't like something in your plan. After the meeting of the creditors, you attend a hearing before a bankruptcy judge who either confirms or denies your plan. If your plan is confirmed, and you make all the payments called for under your plan, you often receive a discharge of any balance owed at the end of your case.

4. Will filing for bankruptcy stop the barrage of collection calls?

Yes. When you file for bankruptcy, something called an "automatic stay" goes into effect. The automatic stay immediately stops collection efforts by your creditors, including harassing phone calls, the prosecution of any lawsuit filed against you, a wage garnishment, an eviction, a foreclosure, a repossession or a seizure of your property by the IRS. (The IRS can continue an audit or issue a tax assessment, however.) A creditor who violates the automatic stay may be fined by the bankruptcy court. A creditor who does not the think the automatic stay is serving its purpose—to freeze your assets so the court can deal with them—can ask the court to "lift" the stay and be allowed to continue collection action.

5. What debts can't be discharged in bankruptcy?

The following debts are nondischargeable in both Chapter 7 and Chapter 13. If you file for Chapter 7, these will remain when your case is over. If you file for Chapter 13, these debts will have to be paid in full during your plan. If they are not, the balance of these debts will remain at the end of your case:

- debts you forget to list in your bankruptcy papers, unless the creditor somehow learns of your bankruptcy case
- child support and alimony
- debts for personal injury or death caused by your intoxicated driving
- student loans for which the first payment became due within the past seven years (plus any time you were granted a deferment or forbearance), unless it would be an undue hardship to repay the loan
- fines and penalties imposed for violating the law, such as traffic tickets and criminal restitution, and
- recent income tax debts and all other kinds of tax debts.

In addition, the following debts may be declared nondischargeable by a bankruptcy judge in Chapter 7 if the creditor challenges your request to discharge them. These debts may be discharged in Chapter 13. You can include them in your plan—at the end of your case, the balance is wiped out:

- debts you incurred on the basis of fraud, such as lying on a credit application
- credit purchases of $1,000 of more for luxury goods or services made within 60 days of filing
- loans or cash advances of $1,000 or more taken within 60 days of filing
- debts from willful or malicious injury to another person or another person's property
- debts from embezzlement, larceny or breach of trust, and
- debts owed under a divorce decree or settlement unless you cannot pay the debts after bankruptcy or the benefit you'd receive by the discharge outweighs any detriment to your ex-spouse.

6. What property might I lose if I file for bankruptcy?

You lose no property in Chapter 13. In Chapter 7, you select property you are eligible to keep from either a list of state exemptions or exemptions provided in the federal Bankruptcy Code. Most debtors use the exemptions provided by their state.

Exemptions are generally as follows:

- Equity in your home, called a homestead exemption. Under the Bankruptcy Code, you can exempt up to $15,000. Some states have no homestead exemption; others allow debtors to protect all or most of the equity in their home.
- Insurance. You usually get to keep the cash value of your policies.
- Pensions. Pensions which qualify under the Employee Retirement Income Security Act (ERISA) are fully protected in bankruptcy. So are many other retirement benefits; often, however, IRAs and Keoghs are not.
- Personal property. You'll be able to keep most household goods, furniture, furnishings, clothing (other than furs), appliances, books and musical instruments. You may be limited up to $1,000 or so in how much jewelry you can keep. Most states let you keep a vehicle worth no more than $1,200 (some states go up to $2,400). And many states give you a "wild card" amount of money—often $1,000 or more—that you can apply toward any property.
- Public benefits. All public benefits, such as welfare, Social Security, unemployment insurance and the like, are fully protected.
- Tools used on the job. You'll probably be able to keep up to a few thousand dollars worth of the tools used in your trade or profession.
- Wages. In most states, you can protect at least 75% of earned but unpaid wages.

7. Why choose Chapter 13 over Chapter 7?

Although the overwhelming number of people who file for bankruptcy choose Chapter 7, there are several reasons why people select Chapter 13:

- You cannot file for Chapter 7 bankruptcy if you received a Chapter 7 or Chapter 13 discharge within the previous six years. Chapter 13 has no such restriction.
- You have valuable nonexempt property.
- You're behind on your mortgage or car loan. In Chapter 7, you'll have to give up the property or pay for it in full during your bankruptcy case. In Chapter 13, you can repay the arrears through your plan, and then keep the

property by making the payments required under the contract. The number one reason people file for Chapter 13 is to stop a home foreclosure, make up the missed payments and get back on track under a home loan agreement.

- You have debts that cannot be discharged in Chapter 7. The second most common reason people file for Chapter 13 is to pay off an IRS debt.
- You have codebtors on personal (nonbusiness) loans. In Chapter 7, the creditors will go after your codebtors for payment. In Chapter 13, the creditors may not seek payment from your codebtors for the duration of your case.
- You feel a moral obligation to repay your debts, you want to learn money management or you hope your creditors might be more inclined to grant you credit after a Chapter 13 than they would after a Chapter 7.

For More Help

How to File for Bankruptcy, by Stephen Elias, Albin Renauer and Robin Leonard (Nolo Press), is a complete guide to filing for Chapter 7 bankruptcy, including all the forms you need.

Nolo's Law Form Kit: Personal Bankruptcy, by Stephen Elias, Albin Renauer, Robin Leonard and Lisa Goldoftas (Nolo Press), contains all the forms and instructions necessary for filing a Chapter 7 bankruptcy.

Chapter 13 Bankruptcy: Repay Your Debts, by Robin Leonard (Nolo Press), contains the forms and instructions necessary to file your own Chapter 13 bankruptcy.

12. Rebuilding Credit

People who have been through a financial crisis—bankruptcy, repossession, foreclosure, history of late payments, IRS lien or levy or something similar—may think they won't ever get credit again. Not true. Following some simple steps, you can rebuild your credit in just a couple of years.

1. What's the first step in rebuilding credit?

To avoid getting into financial problems in the future, you must understand your flow of income and expenses. Some people call this "making a budget." Others find the term budget too restrictive and use the term "spending plan." Whatever you call it, spend at least two months writing down every expenditure. At month's end, compare your total expenses with your income. If you're overspending, you have to cut back or find more income. As best you can, plan how you'll spend your money each month. If you have trouble putting together your own budget, consider getting help from a nonprofit group such as Consumer Credit Counseling Service, which provides budgeting help for free or at a low cost.

2. Okay, I've made my budget. What do I do next?

Now it's time to clean up your credit file. Credit files are compiled by credit bureaus—private, profit-making companies that gather information about a person's credit history and sell it to banks, mortgage lenders, credit unions, credit card companies, department stores, insurance companies, landlords and even a few employers.

Credit bureaus get most of their data from creditors. They also search court records for lawsuits, judgments and bankruptcy filings. And they go through county records to find recorded liens (legal claims).

To create a credit file for a given person, a credit bureau searches its computer files until it finds entries that match the name, Social Security number and any other available identifying information. All matches are gathered together to make the file (or report).

Non-credit data gathered in a credit file usually includes your name, past and present addresses, Social Security number, employment history, marriages and divorces. The bulk of information in a file is your credit history. This includes the name of your creditors, the type and number of each account, when each account was opened, your payment history for the previous 24–36 months, your credit limit or the original amount of a loan and your current balance. The file will show if any accounts have been turned over to a collection agency or if you are disputing a charge.

There are three major credit bureaus—Equifax (headquartered in Atlanta, GA), Trans Union (Chicago, IL) and TRW (Orange, CA). Together they have over 1,000 branches throughout the country. Each company maintains information on nearly 180 million adults living in the U.S.

3. How can I get a copy of my credit file?

The Fair Credit Reporting Act (FCRA) entitles you to a obtain a copy of your credit file. It's free if:

- You've been denied credit because of information in your credit file. You must request your copy within 60 days of being denied credit.

- You haven't requested a copy in the last year. You can get a free copy of your credit file once a year from TRW (TRW Complimentary Report Request, P.O. Box 2350, Chatsworth, CA 91313-2350).

If you haven't been denied credit, you'll have to pay a fee of about $8 to obtain a file from Equifax (P.O. Box 740241, Atlanta, GA 30374-0241) or Trans Union (P.O. Box 390, Springfield, PA 19064), or a second copy within one year from TRW (P.O. Box 949, Allen, TX 75002-0949).

Send the following information:
- your full name (including generations such as Jr., Sr., III)
- your birth date
- your Social Security number,
- your spouse's name
- your telephone number, and
- your current address and addresses for the previous five years.

4. What should I do if there are mistakes in my file?

As you read through your file, make a list of everything out-of-date:
- Lawsuits, paid tax liens, accounts sent out for collection, criminal records and any other adverse information older than seven years.
- Bankruptcies older than ten years. Credit bureaus can count the ten years from the discharge or dismissal, but most count the ten years from the filing. Also, credit bureaus generally include Chapter 13 bankruptcies for only seven years.
- Credit inquiries (requests by companies for a copy of your file) older than two years.

Next, look for incorrect or misleading information, such as:
- incorrect or incomplete name, address, phone number, Social Security number or employment information
- bankruptcies not identified by their specific chapter number
- accounts not yours or lawsuits in which you were not involved
- incorrect account histories—such as late payments when you paid on time
- closed accounts listed as open—it may look as if you have too much open credit, and
- any account you closed that doesn't say "closed by consumer"; otherwise it looks like the creditor closed the account.

Once you compile your list, complete the "request for reinvestigation" form the credit bureau sent you. If the bureau didn't enclose a form, send a letter listing each incorrect item and explain exactly what is wrong. Keep a copy of your request for reinvestigation.

Once the credit bureau receives your request, it must reinvestigate the listings and contact you within 30 days. If you don't hear from the bureau within 30 days, send a follow-up letter. If you let them know that you're trying to obtain a mortgage or car loan, they can do a "rush" verification.

If you are right, or if the creditor who provided the information can no longer verify it, the credit bureau must remove the information from your file. Often credit bureaus will remove an item on request without an investigation if rechecking the item is more bother than it's worth.

If the credit bureau insists that the information is correct, call the credit bureau at its toll-free number to discuss the problem:

- TRW: 800-392-1122
- Trans Union: 800-851-2674
- Equifax: 800-685-1111.

If you don't get anywhere with the credit bureau, directly contact the creditor and ask that the information be removed. Write to the customer service department, vice president of marketing and president or CEO. If the information was reported by a collection agency, send the agency a copy of your letter, too. Be sure to keep a copy of your letter.

If you feel a credit bureau is wrongfully including information in your file, or you want to explain a particular entry, you have the right to put a 100-word statement in your file. The credit bureau must give a copy of your statement—or a summary—to anyone who requests your file. Be clear and concise; use the fewest words possible.

5. What else can I do to rebuild my credit?

After you've cleaned up your credit file, the key to rebuilding credit is to get positive information into your record. Here are a few suggestions:

- If your credit file is missing accounts you pay on time, send the credit bureaus a recent account statement and copies of canceled checks showing your payment history. Ask that these be added to your file. The credit bureau doesn't have to add these accounts, but often will.
- Creditors like to see evidence of stability, so if any of the following information is not in your file, send it to the bureaus and ask that it be added: your current employment; your previous employment (especially if you've been at your current job fewer than two years); your current residence; your telephone number (especially if it's unlisted); your date of birth; your checking or savings account number. Again, the credit bureau doesn't have to add these, but often will.

6. I've been told that I need to use credit to rebuild my credit. Is this true?

Yes. The one type of positive information creditors like to see in credit files is credit payment history. If you have a credit card, use it every month. (Make small purchases and pay them off on time to avoid interest charges.) If you don't have a credit card, apply for one. If you are rejected for a traditional card, apply for a secured card—where you deposit some money into a savings account and then get a credit card with a line of credit around the amount you deposited. If you'd prefer not to apply for a secured card, try to find a cosigner for a traditional credit card.

7. How long does it take to rebuild credit?

If you follow the steps outlined above, it will take about two years to rebuild your credit to the point that you won't be turned down for a major credit card or loan. And after around four years, you may be able to qualify for a mortgage.

For More Help

Money Troubles: Legal Strategies to Cope With Your Debts, by Robin Leonard (Nolo Press), explains your legal rights and offers practical strategies for dealing with debts and creditors.

Nolo's Law Form Kit: Rebuild Your Credit, by Robin Leonard (Nolo Press), provides over a dozen strategies for cleaning up your credit file.

How to Get Out of Debt, Stay Out of Debt, & Live Prosperously, by Jerrold Mundis (Bantam) explains how to live—happily—without credit.

The Federal Trade Commission, 6th & Pennsylvania Ave., NW, Washington, DC 20850, 202-326-2222, publishes free pamphlets on debts and credit, including *Building a Better Credit Record, Buying and Borrowing: Cash in on the Facts, Cosigning a Loan, Credit and Older Americans, Credit Billing Errors, Credit Practices Rule, Equal Credit Opportunity, Fair Credit Billing, Fair Credit Reporting, Fix Your Own Credit Problems and Save Money, Getting a Loan: Your Home as Security, Lost or Stolen Credit and ATM Cards, Solving Credit Problems* and *Women and Credit Histories*.

The Federal Deposit Insurance Corporation, 550 17th St., NW, Washington, DC 20429, 202-393-8400, publishes free pamphlets about credit, including *Equal Credit Opportunity and Age, Fair Credit Billing, Fair Credit Reporting Act* and *How the Equal Credit Opportunity Act Affects You.*

13. WILLS

Though most people are aware that they need a will, the majority of Americans—about 70% of us—don't have one. There are lots of reasons we put off making our wills, from fear of lawyers' fees to fear of death. But writing a will doesn't have to be expensive, or even terribly complicated. And once it's done, you can rest a little easier, knowing that your wishes are known and will be followed after your death.

1. What happens if I die without a will?

If you don't make a will, or use some other legal method to transfer your property when you die, state law will determine what happens to your property. (This process is called "intestate succession.") Your property will be distributed to your spouse and children or, if you have neither, to your other relatives according to a statutory formula. If no relatives can be found to inherit your property by law, it will go into your state's coffers (called "escheating"). Also, in the absence of a will, a court will determine who will care for your children and their property, as well as who will supervise the distribution of the property you leave behind.

2. Do I need a lawyer to make my will?

Probably not. Making a will rarely involves complicated legal rules—most people can draft their own will without any aid other than a good self-help book or software program. If you know what you own, whom you care about, and you have a good self-help resource to guide you, it's hard to make a mistake.

But you shouldn't approach the task of will drafting with a rule against consulting a lawyer. In some situations a lawyer's services are warranted. Even so, you don't have to turn over the whole project; you can simply ask your questions and then finish making your own will. You may want to consult a lawyer if:

- You have questions about your will or other options for leaving your property.
- You expect to leave a very large amount of assets (say, over $1 million) and they will be subject to a substantial estate tax unless you engage in tax planning (but first look at a good self-help resource that discusses tax-savings strategies).
- Rather than simply choosing people to inherit your property, you want to make more complex plans for what happens to it—for example, leaving your house in trust to your spouse until he or she dies and then having it pass to your children. Older people who have remarried often want to set up this type of trust.
- You own a small business and have questions as to the rights of surviving owners or your ownership share.
- You must make arrangements for long-term care of a beneficiary—for example, an incapacitated or disadvantaged child.
- You fear someone will contest your will on grounds of fraud, or claim that you were unduly influenced or weren't of sound mind when you signed it.
- You wish to disinherit, or substantially disinherit, your spouse. It's usually not possible to do this unless you live in a community property state where your spouse already owns half of most assets acquired after marriage. But a

lawyer can help you reduce your spouse's share to the minimum allowed by law.

Also, some people simply feel more comfortable having a lawyer review their will, even though their situation has no apparent legal complications.

3. I don't have much property. Can't I just make a handwritten will?

Handwritten wills, called "holographic" wills, are legal in about 25 states. To be valid, a holographic will must be written, dated and signed in the handwriting of the person making the will. Some states allow will writers to use pre-printed forms if the material provisions of the will are handwritten and the will is properly dated and signed. If you really have very little property, and you want to make just a few specific bequests, a holographic will is better than nothing. But generally, we don't recommend them. Unlike regular wills, holographic wills are not usually witnessed, so if your will goes before a probate court, the court may doubt the reliability of your will and be unusually strict when examining it. It's probably better to take a little extra time to write a will that will easily pass muster when the time comes.

4. How can I be sure my will is legal?

Drafting a valid will isn't nearly as complicated as most people fear. Any adult of sound mind is entitled to make a will. Beyond that, there are just a few technical requirements:

- The will must be typewritten or computer generated (unless it is a valid holographic will, as discussed in Question 3), and expressly state that it's your will.
- You must date and sign the will
- The will must be signed by at least two, or in some states, three, witnesses who watch you sign the will. They must be persons who won't inherit anything under the will.

You don't have to have your will notarized. In many states, though, if you and your witnesses sign an affidavit (sworn statement) before a notary public, you can help simplify the probate court procedures required for the will after you die.

5. Do I need to file my will with a court or in public records somewhere?

No. A will doesn't need to be recorded or filed with any government agency, although it can be in a few states.

6. Can I use my will to name somebody to care for my young children, in case my spouse and I both die suddenly?

Yes. If both parents of a young child die, another adult—called a "personal guardian"—must step in. You and the child's other parent can use your wills to nominate someone to fill this position. To avert conflicts, you should each name the same person. If a guardian is needed, a judge will appoint your nominee as long as he or she agrees that it is in the best interest of your children.

The personal guardian will be responsible for raising your children until they become legal adults. As a matter of common sense, you should have complete confidence in the person you nominate, and you should be certain that your nominee is willing to accept the responsibility of raising your children should the need actually arise.

7. Can I leave property to my young children? Who will manage it for them?

Except for property of little value, the law requires that an adult manage property inherited by children until they turn 18. You can use your will to name someone to manage property inherited by minors, thus avoiding the need for a more complicated court-appointed guardianship. There are many ways to structure a property management arrangement. Here are four of the simplest and most useful:

- **Name a custodian under the Uniform Transfers to Minors Act.** The Uniform Transfers to Minors Act (UTMA) is a law that has been adopted in almost the same form in almost every state. Under the UTMA, you can choose someone, called a custodian, to manage property you are leaving to a child. If you die when the child is under the age set by your state's law—18 in a few states, 21 in most, 25 in several others—the custodian will step in to manage the property. An UTMA custodianship must end by the age specified by your state's law (18, 21 or 25). If you don't trust your beneficiary to manage the property wisely, and you want to extend property management beyond the age set by your state, you may want to use one of the next three methods.

- **Set up a trust for each child.** You can use your will to name someone (called a trustee), who will handle any property the child inherits until the child reaches the age you specify. When the child reaches the age you specified, the trustee ends the trust and gives whatever is left of the trust property to the beneficiary.

- **Set up a "pot trust" for your children.** If you have young children, you may want to set up just one trust for all of them. This arrangement is called a pot trust. In your will, you authorize the trust and appoint a trustee. The trustee doesn't have to spend the same amount on each child; instead, the trustee decides what each child needs, and spends money accordingly. When the youngest child reaches a certain age, usually 18, the trust ends.

- **Name a property guardian.** If you wish, you can simply use your will to name a property guardian for your child. Then, if at your death your child needs the guardian, the court will appoint the person you chose. The property guardian will manage whatever property the child inherits, from you or others, if there's no mechanism (a trust, for example) to handle it.

8. Can I disinherit relatives I don't like?

It depends on whom you want to disinherit. If it's anyone other than your spouse or child, the rule is very simple: don't mention that person in your will, and he or she won't receive any of your property. Rules for spouses and children are somewhat more complex:

Spouses. It is not usually possible to disinherit your spouse completely. If you live in a community property state (Arizona, California, Idaho, Nevada, New Mexico, Texas, Washington or Wisconsin), your spouse automatically owns half of all the property and earnings acquired by either of you during your marriage—there's nothing you can do to change that. You can, however, leave your half of the community property, and your separate property, to anyone you choose.

In all other states, there is no rule that property acquired during marriage is owned by both spouses. To protect spouses from being disinherited, these states give your spouse the right to claim a portion of your estate, no matter what your will provides. But keep in mind that these provisions kick in only if your spouse challenges your will. If your will leaves your spouse less than the statutory share, and he or she doesn't object, the document will be honored as written.

If you don't plan to leave at least half of your property to your spouse in your will and have not provided for him or her generously outside your will, you should consult a lawyer—unless your spouse willingly consents in writing to your plan.

Children. Generally, it's legal to disinherit a child. Some states, however, protect minor children against the loss of a family residence. For example, the Florida constitution prohibits the head of a family from leaving his residence to anyone other than a spouse if he is survived by a spouse or minor child.

Most states have laws—called "pretermitted heir" statutes—to protect children of any age from being accidentally disinherited. If a child is neither named in your will or specifically disinherited, these laws assume that you accidentally forgot to include that child. (In many states, these laws apply only to children born after you made your will, but in some states they apply to any child not mentioned in your will.) The overlooked child has a right to the same share of your estate as he or she would have received if you'd left no will. The share usually depends on whether you leave a spouse and on how many other children you have, but it is likely to be a significant percentage of your property. In some states, these laws apply not only to your children, but also to any of your grandchildren by a child who has died.

To avoid any legal battles after your death, if you decide to disinherit a child, or the child of a deceased child, expressly state this in your will. And if you have a new child after you've made your will, remember to make a new will to include, or specifically disinherit, that child.

9. What happens to my will when I die?

After you die, your executor (the person you appointed in your will) will supervise the process of carrying out your wishes as directed by your will. He or she may hire an attorney to take care of the legal process of winding up your affairs, especially if probate court proceedings are required. Probate is discussed in more detail in the next series of questions.

10. What if someone challenges my will after I die?

Very few wills are ever challenged in court. When they are, it's usually by a close relative who feels somehow cheated out of his or her rightful share of the deceased person's property.

Generally speaking, only spouses are legally entitled to a share of your property (how much depends on state law). Your children aren't entitled to anything unless they show that you unintentionally overlooked them in your will. (See Question 8, above.)

To get an entire will thrown out as invalid, someone must go to court and prove that it suffers from a fatal flaw: the signature was forged, or you weren't of sound mind when you made the will, or you were unduly influenced by someone.

For More Help

WillMaker (Nolo Press) (software for Windows or Macintosh) lets you create a valid will, healthcare directives and final arrangements document using your computer.

The Quick and Legal Will Book, by Denis Clifford (Nolo Press), contains forms and instructions for creating a basic will.

Nolo's Simple Will Book, by Denis Clifford (Nolo Press), contains a detailed discussion of wills and all the forms you need to create one.

Nolo's Law Form Kit: Wills (Nolo Press), contains a simple fill-in-the-blanks will.

Write Your Will (Nolo Press), an audiotape by Ralph Warner.

14. PROBATE AND PROBATE AVOIDANCE

When a person dies, everything stops in connection with his or her affairs, and someone must step in and take charge of things until the estate is settled and the property transferred to its new owners. If a probate court proceeding is required, this process can take many months.

1. What is probate?

Probate is a legal process that includes:

- proving in court that a deceased person's will is valid (usually a routine matter)
- identifying and inventorying the deceased person's property.
- having the property appraised
- paying off legal debts, including death taxes, and
- distributing the remaining property as the will directs.

For the most part, probate involves paperwork and court appearances by lawyers, who are paid from estate property that would otherwise be available to the people named in the will (beneficiaries). The probate process typically drags on for well over a year. Property left by the will cannot be distributed to beneficiaries until the process is complete.

Probate rarely benefits your beneficiaries, and it certainly costs them money and time. Probate makes sense only if your estate will have very complicated problems, such as many debts that can't easily be paid from the property you leave.

2. Who is responsible for handling probate?

In most circumstances, the executor named in the will takes this job. If there wasn't any will, the probate court will name someone to handle probate—most often the closest capable relative, or the person who will inherit the bulk of the deceased person's estate.

Sometimes, no formal probate proceeding is necessary. This may happen if an estate is very small, has been planned using probate avoidance devices such as joint tenancy or a living trust, or because the estate goes mostly to the surviving spouse. In these circumstances, no administrator is formally appointed. Instead, a close relative, often the person who inherits the bulk of the estate, serves as an informal estate representative. Normally, families and friends decide this among themselves, and it is not uncommon for several people to share the responsibility.

3. Is it difficult to serve as estate representative?

Serving as an estate representative can be a tedious job, but it doesn't require special financial or legal knowledge. Common sense, conscientiousness and honesty are the main requirements. If an executor needs help, he or she will be able to hire lawyers, accountants or other experts, and pay them from the assets of the deceased person's estate.

Essentially, the estate representative's job is to protect the deceased person's property until all debts and taxes have been paid, and see that what's left is transferred to the people who are entitled to it. The law does not require an executor to be an expert or to display more than reasonable prudence and judgment, but it does require the highest degree of honesty, impartiality and diligence. This is called a "fiduciary duty"—the duty to act with scrupulous good faith and candor.

4. Does the person named in a will as executor have to serve?

No. When it comes time, an executor can choose whether or not to accept this responsibility. And even if the deceased person's choice does agree to serve, he or she can resign at any time. If an executor decides not to serve or resigns, an alternate named in the will takes over. If no one is available, the court will appoint someone else to step in.

5. What exactly does the executor do?

The executor usually must:

- Decide whether or not probate court proceedings are needed. If the deceased person's property is worth less than a certain amount (it depends on state law), formal probate may not be required.
- Figure out who inherits property. If the deceased person left a will, the executor will read it to determine who gets what. If there's no will, the administrator will have to look at state law (called "intestate succession" statutes) to find out who the deceased person's heirs are.
- Decide whether or not it's legally permissible to transfer certain items immediately to the people named to inherit them, even if probate is required for other property.
- File the will (if any) and all required legal papers in the local probate court, if probate is required.
- Find the deceased person's assets and manage them during the probate process, which commonly takes about a year. This may involve deciding whether to sell real estate or securities owned by the deceased person.
- Handle day-to-day details, such as terminating leases and credit cards, and notifying banks and government agencies—such as Social Security, the post office, Medicare and the Veterans Administration—of the death and the fact that he or she is winding up the person's affairs.
- Set up an estate bank account to hold money that is owed to the deceased person—for example, paychecks or stock dividends.
- Pay continuing expenses—for example, mortgage payments, utility bills and homeowner's insurance premiums.
- Pay debts. As part of this process, the executor must officially notify creditors of the probate proceeding (state law sets out a procedure to follow). Creditors then have about four to six months to file claims.
- Pay taxes. A final income tax return must be filed, covering the period from the beginning of the tax year to the date of death. State and federal estate tax returns may also be required; whether any tax is due will depend on how much property the deceased person owned at death and to whom the property was left.
- Supervise the distribution of the deceased person's property to the people or organizations named in the will.

6. Does the executor get paid?

Obviously, the main reason for serving as a personal representative is to honor the deceased person's request. But the executor is also entitled to payment. The exact amount is regulated by state law and is affected by factors such as the value of the deceased person's property and what the probate court decides is reasonable under the circumstances. Commonly, close relatives (especially those who will inherit a substantial amount under the will) and close friends don't charge the estate for their services.

7. Is a lawyer necessary?

Not always. An executor should definitely consider handling the paperwork without a lawyer if he or she is the main beneficiary, the deceased person's property consists of common kinds of assets (house, bank accounts, insurance), the will seems straightforward, and there are good self-help materials at hand. Essentially, shepherding a case through probate court requires shuffling a lot of papers. A personal representative probably won't ever see the inside of a courtroom; instead, he or she will deal with the court clerk's office. In the vast majority of cases, there are no disputes that require a decision by a judge. The executor may even be able to do everything by mail. Doing a good job requires persistence and attention to tedious detail, but not necessarily a law degree.

But if the estate has many types of property, significant tax liability or potential disputes among inheritors, an executor may want some help.

There are basically two ways for an executor to get help from a lawyer:

- Hire a lawyer to act as a "coach," answering legal questions as they come up. The lawyer might also do some research, look over documents before the executor files them or prepare an estate tax return.
- Turn the probate over to the lawyer. If the executor just doesn't want to deal with the probate process, he or she can hire a lawyer to do everything. The lawyer will be paid out of the estate. In most states, lawyers charge by the hour ($150–$200 is common) or charge a lump sum. In a few places, however, a fee is authorized by state law. For example, in California and a few other states, the law authorizes the lawyer to take a certain percentage of the gross value of the deceased person's estate unless the executor makes a written agreement calling for less. An executor can probably find a competent lawyer who will agree to a lower fee.

8. If an executor doesn't want to hire a lawyer, is there any other way to get help?

Lawyers aren't the only place to get information and assistance. Here are some others:

- **The court.** Probate court clerks will probably answer basic questions about court procedure, but they staunchly avoid saying anything that could possibly be construed as "legal advice." Some courts, however, have lawyers on staff who look over probate documents; they may point out errors in the papers and explain how to fix them.
- **Other professionals.** For certain tasks, an executor may be better off hiring an accountant or appraiser than a lawyer. For example, a CPA may be a big help on some estate tax matters.
- **Paralegals.** In many law offices, lawyers delegate all the probate paperwork to paralegals (non-lawyers who have some training or experience in preparing legal documents). Now, in some areas of the country, experienced paralegals have set up shop to help people directly with probate paperwork. These paralegals don't offer legal advice; they just prepare documents as the executor instructs them. They can also file papers with the court. To find a probate paralegal, an executor can look in the Yellow Pages under "Typing Services" or "Attorney Services." The executor

should hire someone only if that person has substantial experience in this field and provides references to be checked out.

9. Wouldn't it be better to try to avoid probate altogether?

Whether to spend your time and effort planning to avoid probate depends on a number of factors, most notably your age, your health and the size of your estate. If you're young and in good health, a simple will may be all you need—adopting a complex probate avoidance plan now may mean you'll have to re-do it as your life situation changes. And if you have very little property, you might not want to spend your time planning to avoid probate. Your property may even fall under your state's probate exemption (most states have laws that allow a certain amount of property to pass free of probate, or through a simplified probate procedure).

But if you're older (say, over 50), in ill health or own a significant amount of property, you'll probably want to do some planning to avoid probate.

10. What is the best way to avoid probate?

There's no one answer for all people; it depends on your personal and financial situation. The most common probate avoidance methods are:

- **Pay-on-death designations.** Designating a pay-on-death beneficiary is a simple way to avoid probate for bank accounts, government bonds, individual retirement accounts and, in many states, stocks and other securities. In some states, you can even transfer your car through such an arrangement. All you need to do is name someone to inherit the property at your death. You retain complete control of your property when you are alive. Then, when you die, the property is transferred to the person you named, free of probate.
- **Joint tenancy.** Joint tenancy is a form of shared ownership where the surviving owner(s) automatically inherits the share of the owner who dies. Joint tenancy is often a good choice for couples who purchase property together and want the survivor to inherit. (Some states also have a very similar type of ownership, called "tenancy by the entirety" just for married couples.) Generally, it's not a good idea to use joint tenancy as a will substitute because a joint tenant becomes an immediate co-owner and can sell or borrow against his or her share. Also, there are negative tax

consequences of giving appreciated property to a joint tenant shortly before death.

- **A living trust.** A revocable living trust is a popular probate avoidance device. You create the trust by preparing and signing a trust document. Once the trust is created, it has the legal capacity to own property, and you can transfer property to it. When you create a living trust, you don't have to give up any control over the trust property. When you die, the trust property can be distributed directly to the beneficiaries you named in the trust document, without the blessing of the probate court. Living trusts are discussed in more detail in the next series of questions.

- **Insurance.** If you buy life insurance, you can designate a specific beneficiary in your policy. The proceeds of the policy won't go through probate unless you name your own estate as the beneficiary.

- **Gifts.** Anything you give away during your life doesn't have to go through probate. Making non-taxable gifts (up to $10,000 per recipient per year, or to a tax-exempt entity) can also reduce eventual federal estate taxes. So if you can afford it, a gift-giving program can save on both probate costs and estate taxes.

For More Help

The Executor's Handbook, by Theodore E. Hughes and David Klein (Facts On File), is a general but useful guide to an executor's duties. It's not a how-to book, but it discusses many aspects of the executor's job, including funerals, wills, the probate court process, simplified procedures for small estates and managing assets.

How to Probate an Estate in California, by Julia Nissley (Nolo Press), leads you through the California probate process step by step. It contains tear-out copies of all necessary court forms, and instructions for filling them out. Although the forms are used only in California, the book contains much information that would be valuable background in any state.

Social Security, Medicare and Pensions, by Joseph Matthews (Nolo Press) explains Social Security claims.

Plan Your Estate, by Denis Clifford and Cora Jordan (Nolo Press), is a detailed guide to estate planning, including probate avoidance methods, trusts, death taxes, charitable gifts and other topics.

5 Ways to Avoid Probate (Nolo Press), an audiotape by Ralph Warner.

15. LIVING TRUSTS

If you're considering setting up a living trust to avoid probate, there's no shortage of advice out there—much of it contradictory. Personal finance columnists, lawyers, your Uncle Harry—everybody's got an opinion.

Whether or not a living trust is right for you depends on exactly what you want to accomplish and how much paperwork you're willing to put up with. Living trusts work wonderfully for many people, but not everyone needs one.

1. What is a living trust?

A trust, like a corporation, is an entity that exists only on paper but is legally capable of owning property. A flesh-and-blood person, however, must actually be in charge of the property; that person is called the trustee. You can be the trustee of your own living trust, keeping full control over all property legally owned by the trust.

There are many kinds of trusts. A "living trust" (also called an "inter vivos" trust by lawyers who can't give up Latin) is simply a trust you create while you're alive, rather than one that is created at your death.

All living trusts are designed to avoid probate. Some are also designed to help you save on death taxes, and others to manage property.

2. Why do I need a living trust?

If you don't take steps to avoid probate, after your death your property will probably have to detour through court before it reaches the people you want to inherit it. In a nutshell, probate is the court-supervised process of paying your debts and distributing your property to the people entitled to inherit it. (Probate is discussed in more detail in the previous series of questions.)

The average probate drags on for 17 months before the inheritors get anything. And by that time, there's less for them to get: in many cases, about 5% of the property left is eaten up by lawyer and court fees. The exact amount depends on state law and the rates of the lawyer you hire.

3. How does a living trust avoid probate?

Property you transfer into a living trust before your death doesn't go through probate. The successor trustee—the person you appointed to handle the trust after your death—simply transfers ownership to the beneficiaries you named in the trust. In many cases, the whole process takes only a few weeks, and there are no lawyer or court fees to pay. When the property has all been transferred to the beneficiaries, the living trust ceases to exist.

4. Is it expensive to create a living trust?

The expense of a living trust comes up front. Lawyers have figured out that they can charge high fees—much higher than for wills, documents usually of comparable complexity—for living trusts. They commonly charge upwards of $1,000 to draw up a simple trust. If you're going to hire a lawyer to draw up your living trust, you might pay as much now as your heirs would have to pay for probate after your death—which means the trust offers no net savings.

But you don't have to pay a lawyer to create a living trust. With a good self-help book or software program, you can create a valid Declaration of Trust (the document that creates a trust) yourself. If you run into questions that a self-help publication doesn't answer, you may need to consult a lawyer, but you probably won't need to turn the whole job over to an expensive expert.

5. Isn't it a hassle to own property in a trust?

Making a living trust work for you does require some crucial paperwork. You must transfer, in writing, your property to the trust. For example, if you want to leave your house through the trust, you must sign a new deed, showing that you now own the house as trustee of your living trust. This paperwork can be tedious, but the hassles are fewer these days because most institutions are familiar with living trusts.

6. Is a trust document ever made public, like a will?

A will becomes a matter of public record when it is submitted to a probate court, as do all the other documents associated with probate: inventories of the deceased person's assets and debts, for example. The terms of a living trust, however, need not be made public.

7. Does a trust protect property from creditors?

While you're alive, holding assets in a trust doesn't shelter them from creditors. A creditor who wins a lawsuit against you can go after the property in a trust just as if you still owned it in your own name.

After your death, property in a living trust can be quickly and quietly distributed to the beneficiaries (unlike property that must go through probate). That complicates matters for creditors; by the time they find out about your death, your property may already be dispersed, and the creditors have no way of knowing exactly what you owned. It may not be worth the creditor's time and effort to try to track down the property and demand that the new owners use it to pay your debts.

On the other hand, probate can offer a kind of protection from creditors. During probate, creditors must be notified of the death and given a chance to file claims. If they miss the deadline to file, they're out of luck forever.

8. Are there simpler ways to avoid probate?

A living trust isn't the only way to avoid probate. For example, if you and your spouse or partner hold your real estate in joint tenancy, the survivor will inherit the property without probate. You can turn your bank account into a pay-on-death account, through which a beneficiary you name will inherit without probate. In some states, you can register your car or your stocks in a similar transfer-on-death form. And if you don't own much property, it will probably qualify for a simplified, inexpensive probate proceeding under your state's law.

These alternatives have their own drawbacks, and they can't be used in as many situations as a living trust. But they may offer a simpler, cheaper way of avoiding probate's costs and delay.

9. I'm young and healthy. Do I really need a trust now?

Probably not. At this stage in your life, your main estate planning goals are probably making sure that in the unlikely event of your early death, your property is distributed how you want it to be and your young children are cared for. You don't need a trust to accomplish those ends; writing a will, and perhaps buying some life insurance, would be simpler.

10. If I make a trust, do I need a will, too?

Sorry, yes. Having a will is important for several reasons.

First, a will is an essential back-up device for property that you don't transfer to your living trust. For example, if you acquire property shortly before you die, you may not think to transfer ownership of it to your trust—which means that it won't pass under the terms of the trust document. But in your back-up will, you can include a clause that says who should get any property that you don't specifically transfer to your living trust or leave to someone in some other way.

If you don't have a will, any property that isn't transferred by your living trust or other probate avoidance device (such as joint tenancy) will go to your closest relatives in an order determined by state law. These laws are called "intestate succession laws," and they may not distribute property in the way you would have chosen.

11. Can a living trust save on estate taxes?

A simple probate-avoidance living trust has no effect on taxes, but more complicated living trusts can greatly reduce your federal estate tax bill. At present, federal estate taxes are collected from estates valued at $600,000 or more, depending on the year of death.

One more complex living trust is designed primarily for married couples with children. It's commonly called an AB trust, though it goes by many other names, including "credit shelter trust," "exemption trust," "marital life estate trust," "marital bypass trust" and "spousal trust." Spouses put their property in the trust, and then, when one spouse dies, his or her half of the property goes to the children—with the crucial condition that the surviving spouse gets the right to use the deceased spouse's half of the property for life and is entitled to any income it generates. When the second spouse dies, the property goes to the children outright. Using this kind of trust keeps the second spouse's estate half the size it would be if the property were left entirely to the spouse—which means that estate taxes may be avoided altogether.

Unlike a probate-avoidance revocable living trust, an AB trust controls what happens to property for years after the first spouse's death. A couple who makes one must be sure that the surviving spouse will be financially and emotionally comfortable receiving only the income from the money or property placed in trust, with the children as the actual owners of the property.

For More Help

Living Trust Maker (Nolo Press) (software for Windows or Macintosh) lets you make a simple revocable probate-avoidance trust using your computer.

Make Your Own Living Trust, by Denis Clifford (Nolo Press), explains how a living trust can help you avoid probate fees and lower estate taxes and contains forms showing you how to prepare your own living trust.

Plan Your Estate, by Denis Clifford and Cora Jordan (Nolo Press), is a detailed guide to estate planning, including information about living trusts.

16. Estate and Gift Taxes

It's a universal truth that you can't take it with you. But will your estate have to pay for what you leave behind? Most people who consider estate planning are understandably concerned with death taxes (also called estate taxes). The good news is that most peoples' estates won't have to pay any death taxes—federal or state.

1. Will my estate have to pay taxes after I die?

It depends. The federal government imposes estate taxes if your net estate is over a set dollar amount. For a number of years, that amount has been $600,000. But as we go to press, it seems certain that Congress will raise the dollar value of the net amount of property that can pass free of U.S. estate taxes to the following amounts:

Year of Death	Exempt Amount
1996	$625,000
1997	$650,000
1998	$675,000
1999	$700,000
2000	$725,000
2001	$750,000
After 2001	An annual cost-of-living adjustment, rounded to the nearest $10,000.

Most states have abolished death taxes. A minority continue to impose them; the thresholds here vary considerably, from $10,000 or $15,000 to $600,000 or more.

2. What are the rates for federal estate taxes?

The estate tax rate starts at 37% for property worth between $600,000 and $750,000. The maximum is 55% for property worth over $3,000,000.

3. Are there ways to avoid federal estate taxes if it appears my estate will be liable for them?

Yes, although there are fewer ways to avoid estate taxes than many people think, or hope, there are.

The most popular method is frequently used by married couples who plan to leave all or most of their property to each other with the understanding that the property will go to their children after both spouses have died. Rather than leave property to each other outright, the property is left by a trust, commonly called an "AB trust," "exemption trust" or "marital life estate trust." This type of trust can save up to hundreds of thousands of dollars in estate taxes, money that will be passed on to the couple's final inheritors. For more information about how an AB trust works, see Question 11 in the previous set of questions, *Living Trusts*.

4. What other estate tax saving methods are there?

Common ones include what's called a "QTIP" trust, which enables a surviving spouse to postpone estate taxes that would otherwise be due when the other spouse dies. And there are many different types of charitable trusts, some of which can be used to provide both income tax and estate tax advantages. There's also a new estate tax break in the recent Congressional law which allows major estate tax savings for a "family business." Because this is new, and large amounts of money may be involved, the IRS and clever tax lawyers will be struggling with it for some time.

5. What's the rate for state death taxes?

In the states that have them, the tax rates vary widely. In some states, death taxes take only a minor bite from your property. For example, in Connecticut, Iowa, Kansas, Hew Hampshire and a few other states, all property left to a surviving spouse is free of tax, and in Maryland the tax rate for property left to close family members is just 1%. In other states, death taxes can bite off a more sizeable hunk. In New York, for example, the tax on an estate of $700,000 would be about $31,500.

6. Are there ways to avoid paying state death taxes?

If you live in two states—winter here, summer there—your inheritors may save on death taxes if you can make your legal residence in the state with lower, or no, death taxes. But most people have real connections with just one state, and there isn't much they can do if that state imposes death taxes.

7. Can't I just give all my property away before I die and avoid estate taxes?

No. The government long anticipated this one. If you give away more than $10,000 per year to any one person (or non-charitable institution), you are assessed federal "gift tax," which applies at the same rate as the estate tax.

8. But I've heard that people do save on estate taxes by making gifts. How?

You can achieve substantial estate tax savings by making use of the $10,000 annual gift tax exclusion. If you give away $10,000 for four years, you've removed $40,000 from your taxable estate. And each member of a couple has a separate $10,000 exclusion. So a couple can give $20,000 a year to a child free of gift tax. If you have a few children, or other people you want to make gifts to (such as your children's spouses), you can use this method to significantly reduce the size of your taxable estate over a few years. Consider a couple with an combined estate of $1,000,000 who have three children. Each year they give each child $20,000 tax free, or a total of $60,000 per year. In six years, the couple has given away $360,000 and has reduced their estate to $640,000, below the estate tax threshold.

Of course, there are risks with this kind of gift giving program. The most obvious is that you are legally transferring your wealth. Gift giving to reduce eventual estate taxes must be carefully evaluated to see if you can comfortably afford to give away your property during your lifetime.

For More Help

Plan Your Estate, by Denis Clifford and Cora Jordan (Nolo Press), is a detailed guide to estate planning, including all major methods of reducing or avoiding estate and gift taxes.

17. FUNERAL PLANNING AND OTHER FINAL ARRANGEMENTS

A final arrangements document is a set of written instructions you prepare setting out the details of what you want to happen to your body after death, including any ceremonies and observances you wish to have held.

1. Why should I leave written instructions about my final ceremonies and the disposition of my body?

Letting your survivors know what kind of ceremonies and body disposition you want saves them the pain of making such decisions at what is likely to be a difficult time for them.

And many family members and friends have found that discussing preferences for final arrangements is a great relief—especially if a person is elderly or in poor health and death is likely to occur soon.

Planning some of these details in advance can also help save money. For many people, death goods and services are the third most costly expense—just after homes and cars. Advance planning, with some wise comparison shopping, can help ensure that costs will be controlled or kept to a minimum.

2. Why not leave these instructions in my will?

A will is not a good place to express your death and burial preferences for one simple reason: your will probably won't be located and read until several weeks after you die—long after the time such final arrangements must occur.

A will should be reserved for directions on how to divide and distribute your property and, if applicable, who should get care and custody of your children if you die while they're still young.

3. What happens if I don't leave written instructions?

If you die without leaving written instructions about your preferences, state law will determine who will have the right to decide how your remains will be handled. In most states, the right—and the liability for paying for the reasonable costs of disposing of remains—rests with the following people, in order of primary right:

- surviving spouse
- surviving child or children
- surviving parent or parents
- the next of kin, and
- the public administrator, who is appointed by a court.

Most disputes arise where there is more than one person—three children, for example—who disagree over a fundamental decision, such as whether the body of a parent should be buried or cremated. As mentioned, such disputes can be avoided if you are willing to do some planning and to put your wishes in writing.

4. What details should I include in a final arrangements document?

What you choose to include, of course, is a personal matter—likely to be dictated by custom, religious preference or simply your own whims. In a typical final arrangements document, you might include:

- the name of the mortuary or other institution that will handle your burial or cremation
- whether you wish to be embalmed
- the type of casket or container in which you will be buried or cremated, including whether you want it present at any after-death ceremony
- the details of any ceremony you want before the burial or cremation, including specific clothing and jewelry in which you want your body to be attired
- who your pallbearers will be if you wish to have some
- how you will be transported to the cemetery and gravesite
- where your remains will be buried, stored or scattered
- the details of any ceremony you want to accompany your burial, interment or scattering
- the details of any marker you want to show where your remains are buried or interred
- any epitaph you wish placed on your burial marker, and
- the details of any ceremony you want held after you are buried or cremated.

5. What services can I expect from a mortuary?

Most mortuaries or funeral homes are equipped to handle many of the details related to disposing of a person's remains. These include:

- collecting the body from the place of death
- storing the body until it is buried or cremated
- making burial arrangements with a cemetery
- conducting ceremonies related to the burial
- preparing the body for burial, and
- arranging to have the body transported for burial.

6. Where can I turn for help in making final arrangements?

Choosing the institution to handle your burial is probably the most important final arrangement that you can make, from an economic standpoint. For this reason, many people join memorial or funeral societies, which help them find local mortuaries that will deal honestly with their survivors and charge prices that accurately reflect the value of their services.

Society members are free to choose whatever final arrangements they wish. Most societies, however, emphasize simple, dignified arrangements over the costly, elaborate services often promoted by the funeral industry.

While the services offered by each society differ, most societies distribute literature and information on options and legal controls on final arrangements.

Members receive a prearrangement form upon joining, which allows them to plan for the goods and services they want—and to get them for a predetermined cost. Many societies also serve as a watchdogs—making sure that individuals get and pay for only the services they have specified.

The cost for joining these organizations is low—usually from $20 to $40 for a lifetime membership, although some societies periodically charge a small renewal fee.

To find a funeral or memorial society near you, look in the Yellow Pages of your telephone book under Funeral Information and Advisory Services, or contact the Continental Association of Funeral and Memorial Societies, 800-458-5563, for additional information.

7. Should I pay in advance for funeral goods and services?

Shopping around for the most suitable and affordable funeral goods and services is a wise idea. Be extremely cautious, however, about paying in advance—or prepaying—for them.

While there are a number of legal controls on how the funeral industry can handle and invest funds earmarked for future services, there are many reported abuses of mismanaged and stolen funds. A great many other abuses go unreported by family members too embarrassed or too grief-stricken to complain.

There are additional pitfalls. When mortuaries go out of business, the consumer who has prepaid is often left without funds and without recourse. Also, many individuals who move to a new locale during their lifetimes are dismayed to find that their prepayment funds are nonrefundable—or that there is a substantial financial penalty for withdrawing or transferring them. In addition, money paid now may not cover inflated costs of the future—meaning that survivors will be left to cover the substantially inflated costs.

If you are interested in setting aside a fund of money to pay for your final arrangements, a more prudent approach for most people is to set up something called a Totten Trust—a trust or savings plan earmarked to pay for your final arrangements—with a bank or savings institution. Most will do so for a very slight charge, the trust funds are easily transferred or withdrawn if need be and you have complete control over the money during your life.

8. How can I arrange to donate my body for scientific research or study after my death?

Whole body donations must usually be made while you are alive, although some medical schools will accept a cadaver through arrangements made after death.

The best place to contact to arrange a whole body donation is the nearest medical school. There are currently medical schools in every state except for Alaska, Delaware, Idaho, Montana and Wyoming. The medical schools in Arizona, Nebraska, Nevada, South Carolina and Wisconsin have the most strict rules about enrolling in body donation programs before death.

If you live in a state with no medical school or one that has very strict requirements for whole body donations, you may wish to find out more about your body donation options from the National Anatomical Service, which operates 24-hour phone services out of New York, 718-948-2401, and St. Louis, 314-726-9079.

9. How can I arrange to donate my body organs for others to use after my death?

The principal method for donating organs is by indicating your intent to do so on a uniform donor card. Once signed, this card identifies you to medical personnel as a potential organ donor. You can get a donor card or form from most hospitals, the county or state office of the National Kidney Foundation or a community eye bank.

In most states, you can also obtain an organ donation card from the local Department of Motor Vehicles. Depending on where you live, you can check a box, affix a stamp or seal or attach a separate card to your license, indicating your wish to donate one or more organs.

If you fill out an organ donor card, make sure you tell family members you have done so.

Even if you have not signed a card or other document indicating your intent to donate your organs, your next of kin can approve a donation after you die. And conversely, even if you have indicated an intent to donate your organs, an objection by your next of kin will often defeat your intention; medical personnel will usually not proceed in the face of an objection from relatives. The best safeguard is to discuss your wishes with close friends and relatives, emphasizing your strong feelings about donating your body for research or teaching.

For More Help

WillMaker (Nolo Press) (software for Windows or Macintosh) lets you use your computer to create a final arrangements document, in addition to a valid will and healthcare directives.

18. Durable Power of Attorney for Finances

Many of us feel a well-grounded fear that we may someday become seriously ill and unable to handle our own affairs. Who would act on our behalf to pay bills, make bank deposits, watch over investments and deal with the paperwork that accompanies collecting insurance and government benefits?

Preparing a document called a durable power of attorney for finances is a simple, inexpensive and reliable way to ensure that your finances stay in the hands of a trusted person you choose. It's also a wonderful thing to do for your family members. If you do become incapacitated, the durable power of attorney will likely appear as a minor miracle to those close to you.

1. What is a durable power of attorney?

When you create and sign a power of attorney, you give another person legal authority to act on your behalf. The person who is given this authority is called your "attorney-in-fact." The word "attorney" here means anyone authorized to act on another's behalf; it's most definitely not restricted to lawyers.

A "durable" power of attorney stays valid even if you become unable to handle your own affairs (incapacitated). If you don't specify that you want your power of attorney to continue if you become incapacitated, it will automatically end (in almost all states) if you later become incapacitated.

2. When does a durable power of attorney take effect?

A durable power of attorney can be drafted so that it goes into effect as soon as you sign it. That is appropriate if you face a serious operation or incapacitating illness.

You can also specify that the durable power of attorney does not go into effect unless a doctor certifies that you have become incapacitated. This is called a "springing" durable power of attorney. It allows you to keep control over your affairs unless and until you become incapacitated, when it springs into effect.

3. What does the attorney-in-fact do?

Commonly, people give an attorney-in-fact broad power over their finances. But you can give your attorney-in-fact as much or as little power as you wish. You may want to give your attorney-in-fact authority to do some or all of the following:

- use your assets to pay your everyday expenses and those of your family
- buy, sell, maintain, pay taxes on and mortgage real estate and other property
- collect benefits from Social Security, Medicare or other government programs or civil or military service
- invest your money in stocks, bonds and mutual funds
- handle transactions with banks and other financial institutions
- buy and sell insurance policies and annuities for you
- file and pay your taxes
- operate your small business
- claim property you inherit or are otherwise entitled to

- represent you in court or hire someone to represent you, and
- manage your retirement accounts.

Whatever powers you give the attorney-in-fact, the attorney-in-fact must act in your best interests, keep accurate records, keep your property separate from his or hers and avoid conflicts of interest.

4. How do I create a durable power of attorney for finances?

To create a legally valid durable power of attorney, all you need to do is properly complete and sign a fill-in-the-blanks form that's a few pages long. Some states have their own forms.

After you fill out the form, you must sign it in front of a notary public. In some states, witnesses must also watch you sign the document. If your attorney-in-fact will have authority to deal with your real estate, you may also need to put a copy on file at the local land records office.

Some banks and brokerage companies have their own durable power of attorney forms. If you want your attorney-in-fact to have an easy time with these institutions, you may need to prepare two (or more) durable powers of attorney: the bank's form and a broader form.

5. What happens if I don't have a durable power of attorney for finances?

If you become incapacitated and you haven't prepared a durable power of attorney for finances, a court proceeding is probably inescapable. Your spouse, closest relatives or companion will have to ask a court for authority over at least some of your financial affairs.

If you are married, your spouse does have some authority over property you own together—to pay bills from a joint bank account, for example. There are significant limits, however, on your spouse's right to sell property owned by both of you.

If your relatives go to court to get someone appointed to manage your financial affairs, they must ask a judge to rule that you cannot take care of your own affairs—a public airing of a very private matter. And like any court proceeding, it can be expensive if a lawyer must be hired. Depending on where you live, the person appointed is called a conservator, guardian of the estate, committee or curator. When this person is appointed, the incapacitated person loses the right to control his or her own money.

The appointment of a conservator is usually just the beginning of court proceedings. Often the conservator must:

- post a bond—a kind of insurance policy that pays if the conservator steals or misuses property
- prepare (or hire a lawyer or accountant to prepare) detailed financial reports and periodically file them with the court, and
- get court approval for certain transactions, such as selling real estate or making slightly risky investments.

A conservatorship isn't necessarily permanent, but it may be ended only by the court.

6. Isn't a conservatorship sometimes a good idea?

In a few situations, the expense and intrusion of a conservatorship are justified:

- There's no one you trust enough to give broad authority over your property and finances.
- You have a considerable amount of property and fear that family members would fight over its management if you appointed an attorney-in-fact. Your

relatives may still fight, but at least the court will be there to keep an eye on your welfare and your property.

7. I have a living trust. Do I still need a durable power of attorney for finances?

A revocable living trust can be useful if you become incapable of taking care of your financial affairs. That's because the person who will distribute trust property after your death (the successor trustee) can also, in most cases, take over management of the trust property if you become incapacitated.

Few people, however, transfer all their property to a living trust, and the successor trustee has no authority over property that the trust doesn't own. So a living trust isn't a complete substitute for a durable power of attorney for finances.

8. Can my attorney-in-fact make medical decisions on my behalf?

No. A durable power of attorney for finances does *not* give your attorney-in-fact legal authority to make medical decisions for you.

You can, however, prepare a durable power of attorney for healthcare, a document that lets you choose someone to make medical decisions on your behalf if you can't.

In most states, you'll also want to write out your wishes in a "living will" (also called a Healthcare Directive or Directive to Physicians), which will tell your doctors your preferences about certain kinds of medical treatment and life-sustaining procedures if you can't communicate your wishes. If your living will is properly prepared, your doctors are legally bound to respect your wishes or to transfer you to a doctor who will. Most states now provide fill-in-the-blanks living will forms.

Healthcare documents are discussed in more detail in the next series of questions, *Healthcare Directives*.

9. When does the durable power of attorney end?

It ends at your death. That means that you can't give your attorney-in-fact authority to handle things after your death, such as paying your debts, making funeral or burial arrangements or transferring your property to the people who inherit it. If you want your attorney-in-fact to have authority to wind up your affairs after your death, use a will to name that person as your executor.

Your durable power of attorney also ends if you recover sufficiently from your injury or illness and revoke it.

10. Where can I get a durable power of attorney form?

Unfortunately, there is no one good source for current financial power of attorney forms. But here are a couple of places to start:

- About a dozen states (Alaska, California, Colorado, Connecticut, Illinois, Indiana, Minnesota, Montana, New Mexico, New York, North Carolina, Texas and Wisconsin) have their own fill-in-the-blank forms, published in their statute books. You can find your state's form by going to a law library and looking up "Durable Power of Attorney" in the index to the state statutes. Then type out a document, following the model form exactly.
- Banks and other financial institutions sometimes have their own forms to cover just transactions involving them. If you want to give someone authority over your checking account, for example, call your bank and ask if it has its own durable power of attorney form for you to sign.

If you need more help finding or filling out a form for your state, contact a lawyer.

19. HEALTHCARE DIRECTIVES

Nearly 80% of Americans die in a hospital or other care facility. The doctors who work in these facilities are generally charged with preserving a patient's life through whatever means are available. This may or may not be what you would like in the way of treatment. Healthcare directives give you the opportunity to write out your wishes in advance and ensure some legal respect for them if ever you are unable to speak for yourself.

1. What is a living will?

A living will, known in some states as a Directive to Physicians or Healthcare Directive, sets out a person's wishes about what medical treatment should be withheld or provided if a person becomes unable to communicate those wishes. The directive creates a contract with the attending doctor. Once the doctor receives a properly signed and witnessed directive, he or she is under a duty either to honor its instructions or to make sure the patient is transferred to the care of another doctor who will honor them.

Healthcare directives aren't used just to instruct doctors to withhold life prolonging treatments. Some people want to reinforce that they would like to receive all medical treatment that is available—a healthcare directive is the proper place to specify that.

2. What is a durable power of attorney for healthcare? Doesn't that do the same thing as a living will?

A durable power of attorney for healthcare—called a Healthcare Proxy in some states—gives another person authority to make medical decisions for you if you are unable to make those decisions for yourself. The document doesn't necessarily state what type of treatment you want to receive (as does a living will)—you can leave those decisions to your proxy if you feel comfortable doing so. Ideally, however, the two documents will work together. For example, your healthcare directive may contain a clause appointing a proxy (sometimes called an attorney-in-fact, agent or representative) to be certain your wishes are carried out as you've directed. Or you may create two separate documents, a directive explaining the treatment you wish to receive and a durable power of attorney appointing someone to oversee your directive.

If you do not know anyone you trust to name as your healthcare proxy, it is still important to complete and finalize a healthcare directive recording your wishes. That way, your doctors will still be obligated to give you the healthcare you want.

3. Can anyone make a healthcare directive?

In most states, you must be 18 years old, though a few states allow parents to make healthcare directives for their minor children.

Every state law requires that the person making a healthcare directive must be able to understand what the document means, what it contains and how it works.

If you are physically disabled you may make a valid healthcare document—simply direct another person to sign the document for you if you are unable to sign it yourself.

4. What happens if I don't have any healthcare documents?

If you have not completed either a formal document such as a healthcare directive to express your wishes, or a durable power of attorney to appoint someone to make healthcare decisions on your behalf, the doctors who attend you will use their own discretion in deciding what kind of medical care you will receive.

When a question arises about whether surgery or some other serious procedure is authorized, doctors may turn for consent to a close relative—spouse, parent or adult child. Friends and unmarried partners, although they may be most familiar with your wishes for your medical treatment, are rarely consulted, or are purposefully left out of the decision-making process.

Problems arise where partners and family members disagree about what treatment is proper. In the most complicated case scenarios, these battles over medical care wind up in court, where a judge, who usually has little medical knowledge and no familiarity with you, is called upon to decide the future of your treatment. Such legal battles—which are costly, time-consuming and usually painful to those involved—are unnecessary if you have the care and foresight to use a formal document to express your wishes for your healthcare.

5. When does my healthcare directive take effect?

Your healthcare directive takes effect when three things happen:

- you are diagnosed to be close to death from a terminal condition or to be permanently comatose
- you cannot communicate your own wishes for your medical care—orally, in writing or through gestures, and
- the medical personnel attending you are notified of your written directions for your medical care.

In most instances, you can ensure that your directive becomes part of your medical record when you are admitted to a hospital or other care facility. But to ensure that your wishes will be followed if your need for care arises unexpectedly or while you are out of your home state or country, it is best to give copies of your completed documents to several people.

6. Who should I choose as a healthcare proxy?

The person you name as your healthcare proxy should be someone you trust—and someone with whom you feel confident discussing your wishes. While your proxy need not agree with your wishes for your medical care, you should believe that he or she respects your right to get the kind of medical care you want.

The person you appoint to oversee your healthcare wishes could be a spouse or partner, relative or close friend. Keep in mind that your proxy may have to fight to assert your wishes in the face of a stubborn medical establishment—and against the wishes of family members who may be driven by their own beliefs and interests, rather than yours. If you foresee the possibility of a conflict in enforcing your wishes, be sure to choose a proxy who is strong-willed and assertive.

While you need not name someone who lives in the same state as you do, proximity should be one factor you consider. The reality is that the person you name may be called upon to spend weeks or months near your bedside, making sure medical personnel abide by your wishes for your healthcare.

You should not choose your doctor, or an employee of a hospital or nursing home where you are receiving treatment. In fact, the laws in many states prevent you from naming such a person. In a few instances, this legal constraint may frustrate your wishes. For example, you may wish to name your spouse or partner as your representative, but if he or she also works as a hospital employee, that alone may bar you from naming that person. If the laws in your state ban your first choice, you may have to name another person to serve instead.

7. What if I really don't know anyone I trust to supervise my medical care?

Naming a healthcare proxy is an optional part of completing your healthcare directive. It is better not to name anyone than to name someone who is not comfortable with the directions you leave—or who is not likely to assert your wishes strongly.

Medical personnel are still technically bound to follow your written wishes for your healthcare—or to find someone who will care for you in the way you have directed. It is far better to put your wishes for final healthcare in writing than to let the lack of a representative stand in the way.

8. What types of medical care should I consider when completing my healthcare documents?

Technological advances mean that currently unfathomable procedures and treatments will become available and treatments that are now common will become obsolete. Also, the treatments that are available vary drastically with region, depending on the sophistication and funding levels of local medical facilities.

While putting together your healthcare directive, the best that you can do is to become familiar with the kinds of medical procedures that are most commonly administered to patients who are terminally ill or permanently comatose. Those most commonly administered include:

- blood and blood products
- cardio-pulmonary resuscitation (CPR)
- diagnostic tests
- dialysis
- drugs
- respirators, and
- surgery.

9. Can I leave instructions about pain medication, or about food and water?

The laws of most states assume that people want relief from pain and discomfort and specifically exclude pain-relieving procedures from definitions of life-prolonging treatments that may be withheld. Some states also exclude food and water (commonly called nutrition and hydration) from their definitions of life-prolonging treatments. But there is some controversy about whether providing food and water, or drugs to make a person comfortable, will also have the effect of prolonging life. Some people are so adamant about not having their lives prolonged when they are comatose or likely to die soon that they choose to direct that all food, water and pain relief be withheld, even if the doctor thinks those procedures are necessary. Under the U.S. Constitution, you are allowed to leave these instructions even if your state's law is restrictive—your doctors should be bound to follow your wishes.

On the other hand, some people feel concerned about how much pain or discomfort might be felt when close to death from a terminal illness or in a permanent coma; these people are willing to have their lives prolonged rather than face the possibility that discomfort or pain would go untreated. Obviously, it's a very personal choice—you're free to leave the instructions that feel right for you.

10. How can I be certain that my healthcare documents are legal?

All states require that you sign your documents—or direct another person to sign them for you—as a way of verifying that you understand them and that they contain your true wishes.

But do not sign them immediately. You must sign your documents in the presence of witnesses or a notary public—sometimes both (this depends on your state's law). The purpose of this additional formality is so that there is at least one other person who can confirm that you were of sound mind and of legal age—usually 18—when you made the documents. Be aware that in some states the requirements for finalizing your healthcare directive will be slightly different from those for finalizing your durable power of attorney for healthcare.

11. Where can I get a healthcare directive—and who can help complete it?

Many people first realize the need for healthcare documents when they're being admitted to a hospital. But hospital admission time is probably not the best time to learn about your options in directing healthcare or to reflect on your wishes—it's better to get information and complete your documents when you're under less stress.

Local senior centers may be good resources for help. Many of them have trained healthcare staff on hand who will be willing to discuss your healthcare options. The patient representative at a local hospital may also be a good person to contact for help. And if you have a regular physician, you can discuss your concerns with him or her.

Local special interest groups and clinics may provide help in obtaining and filling out healthcare directives—particularly organizations set up to meet the needs of the severely ill such as AIDS groups or cancer organizations. Check your telephone book for a local listing—or call one of the group's hotlines for more information or a possible referral.

There are also a number of seminars offered to help people with their healthcare documents. Beware of groups that offer such seminars for a hefty fee, however. Hospitals and senior centers often provide them free of charge.

For More Help

WillMaker (Nolo Press) (software for Windows and Macintosh) walks you step-by-step through the process of writing your own will, healthcare documents and a document setting out your final arrangements.

20. DIVORCE

Divorce is the legal termination of a marriage. In some states, divorce is called dissolution or dissolution of marriage.

1. How does an annulment differ from a divorce?

Like a divorce, an annulment is a court procedure that dissolves a marriage. But an annulment treats the marriage as though it never happened. For some people, divorce carries a stigma, and they would rather their marriage be annulled. Others prefer an annulment because it may be easier to remarry in their church if they go through an annulment rather than a divorce.

Annulments may be obtained for one of the following reasons:

- misrepresentation or fraud (for example, a spouse lied about the capacity to have children, stated that she had reached the age of consent or failed to say that she was still married to someone else)
- concealment (for example, concealing an addiction to alcohol or drugs, conviction of a felony, children from a prior relationship, a sexually transmitted disease or impotency)
- refusal or inability to consummate the marriage—that is, refusal or inability of a spouse to have sexual intercourse with the other spouse, or
- misunderstanding (for example, one person wanted children and the other did not).

These are the grounds for civil annulments; within the Roman Catholic Church, a couple may obtain a religious annulment after obtaining a civil divorce, in order for one or both spouses to remarry.

Most annulments take place after a marriage of a very short duration—a few weeks or months, so there are usually no assets or debts to divide, or children for whom custody, visitation and child support are a concern. When a long-term marriage is annulled, however, most states have provisions for dividing property and debts, and determining custody, visitation and child support and alimony. Children of an annulled marriage are *not* considered illegitimate.

2. When are married people considered separated?

Many people are confused about what is meant by "separated"—and it's no wonder, given that there are four different kinds of separations:

- **Trial Separation.** When a couple lives apart for a test period, to decide whether or not to separate permanently, it's called a trial separation. Even if they don't get back together, the assets they accumulate and debts they incur during the trial period are usually considered jointly owned.
- **Living Apart.** Spouses who no longer reside in the same dwelling are said to be living apart. In some states, living apart without intending to reunite changes the spouses' property rights. For example, some states consider property accumulated and debts incurred between living apart and divorce to be the separate property or debt of the person who accumulated or incurred it.
- **Permanent Separation.** When a couple decides to split up, it's often called a permanent separation. It may follow a trial separation, or may begin immediately when the couple starts living apart. In most states, all assets received and most debts incurred after permanent separation are the separate property or responsibility of the spouse incurring them.

- **Legal Separation.** A legal separation results when the parties separate and a court rules on the division of property, alimony, child support, custody and visitation—but does not grant a divorce. The money awarded for support of the spouse and children under these circumstances is often called separate maintenance (as opposed to alimony and child support).

3. What exactly is a "no fault" divorce?

"No fault" divorce describes any divorce where the spouse suing for divorce does not have to prove that the other spouse did something wrong. All states allow divorces regardless of who is at "fault."

To get a no fault divorce, one spouse must simply state a reason recognized by the state. In most states, it's enough to declare that the couple cannot get along (this goes by such names as "incompatibility," "irreconcilable differences," or "irremediable breakdown of the marriage"). In nearly a dozen states, however, they must have been living apart for a period of months or even years.

4. Is a no fault divorce the only option even when there has been substantial wrongdoing?

In 15 states, yes. The rest allow a spouse to select either a no fault divorce or a fault divorce. Why choose a fault divorce? Some people don't want to wait out the period of separation required by their state's law for a no fault divorce. And in some states, a spouse who proves the other's fault may receive a greater share of the marital property, or more alimony.

The traditional fault grounds are:

- cruelty (inflicting unnecessary emotional or physical pain). This is the most frequently used ground because courts accept minor wrongs as sufficient evidence.
- adultery
- desertion for a specified length of time
- confinement in prison for a set number of years, and
- physical inability to engage in sexual intercourse, if it was not disclosed before marriage.

5. What happens in a fault divorce if both spouses are at fault?

Under a doctrine called "comparative rectitude," a court will grant the spouse least at fault a divorce when both parties have shown grounds for divorce. Years ago, when both parties were at fault, neither was entitled to a divorce. The absurdity of this result gave rise to the concept of comparative rectitude.

6. Can a spouse successfully prevent a court from granting a divorce?

One spouse cannot stop a no fault divorce. Objecting to the other spouse's request for divorce is itself an irreconcilable difference that would justify the divorce.

A spouse can prevent a fault divorce, however, by convincing the court that he or she is not at fault. In addition, several other defenses to a divorce may be possible:

- **Collusion.** If the only no fault divorce available in a state requires that the couple separate for a long time and the couple doesn't want to wait, they might pretend that one of them was at fault in order to manufacture a ground for divorce. This is collusion because they are cooperating in order to mislead the judge. If, before the divorce, one spouse no longer wants a divorce, he could raise the collusion as a defense.

- **Condonation.** Condonation is someone's approval of another's activities. For example, a wife who does not object to her husband's adultery may be said to condone it. If the wife sues her husband for divorce, claiming he has committed adultery, the husband may argue as a defense that she condoned his behavior.

- **Connivance.** Connivance is the setting up of a situation so that the other person commits a wrongdoing. For example, a wife who invites her husband's lover to the house and then leaves for the weekend may be said to have connived his adultery. If the wife sues her husband for divorce, claiming he has committed adultery, the husband may argue as a defense that she connived—that is, set up—his actions.

- **Provocation.** Provocation is the inciting of another to do a certain act. If a spouse suing for divorce claims that the other spouse abandoned her, her spouse might defend the suit on the ground that she provoked the abandonment.

7. Do you have to live in a state to get a divorce there?

Yes. All states require a spouse to be a resident of the state—often for at least six months—before filing for a divorce there. Someone who files for divorce must offer proof that he has resided there for the required length of time.

8. Can one spouse move to a different state or country to get a divorce?

If one spouse meets the residency requirement of a state or country, a divorce obtained there is valid, even if the other spouse lives somewhere else. The courts of all states will recognize the divorce.

Any decisions the court makes regarding property division, alimony, custody and child support, however, may not be valid unless the non-resident spouse consented to the jurisdiction of the court or later acts as if the foreign divorce was valid—for example, by paying court-ordered child support.

9. How is property divided at divorce?

It is common for a divorcing couple to decide about dividing their property and debts themselves, rather than leave it to the judge. But if a couple cannot agree, they may submit their property dispute to the court, which will use state law to divide their property.

Division of property does not necessarily mean a physical division. Rather, the court awards each spouse a percentage of the total value of the property. Each spouse gets items whose worth adds up to his or her percentage.

Courts divide property under one of two schemes: equitable distribution or community property.

- **Equitable Distribution.** Assets and earnings accumulated during marriage are divided equitably (fairly). In practice, often two-thirds of the assets go to the higher wage earner and one-third to the other spouse. Equitable distribution principles are followed everywhere except the community property states listed just below.
- **Community Property.** Arizona, California, Idaho, Louisiana, Nevada, New Mexico, Texas, Washington and Wisconsin follow the community property system. All property of a married person is classified as either community property, owned equally by both spouses, or separate property of one spouse. At divorce, community property is generally divided equally between the spouses, while each spouse keeps his or her separate property.

Very generally, here are the rules for determining what's community property and what isn't:

Community property includes all earnings during marriage and everything acquired with those earnings. All debts incurred during marriage, unless the creditor was specifically looking to the separate property of one spouse for payment, are community property debts.

Separate property of one spouse includes gifts and inheritances given just to that spouse, personal injury awards received by that spouse, and the proceeds of a pension that vested (that is, the pensioner became legally entitled to receive it) before marriage.

Property purchased with the separate funds of a spouse remain that spouse's separate property. A business owned by one spouse before the marriage remains his or her separate property during the marriage, although a portion of it may be considered community property if the business increased in value during the marriage or both spouses worked at it.

Property purchased with a combination of separate and community funds is part community and part separate property, so long as a spouse is able to show that some separate funds were used. Separate property that is mixed together with community property generally becomes community property.

For More Help

How to Do Your Own Divorce in California, by Charles Sherman (Nolo Press), contains step-by-step instructions for obtaining a California divorce without a lawyer.

How to Do Your Own Divorce in Texas, by Charles Sherman (Nolo Press), contains step-by-step instructions for obtaining a Texas divorce without a lawyer.

Divorce and Money: How to Make the Best Financial Decisions During Divorce, by Violet Woodhouse and Victoria F. Collins, with M.C. Blakeman (Nolo Press), explains the financial aspects of divorce and how to divide property fairly.

Smart Ways to Save Money During and After Divorce, by Victoria F. Collins and Ginita Wall (Nolo Press), offers tips on how to save money during the divorce process.

Nolo's Pocket Guide to Family Law, by Robin Leonard and Stephen Elias (Nolo Press), explains legal concepts you may run across if you're involved in a divorce, adoption or other family law matter.

Annulment: Your Chance to Remarry Within the Catholic Church, by Joseph P. Zwack (Harper & Row), explains how to get a religious annulment.

21. Child Custody and Visitation

When parents separate or divorce, the term "custody" often serves as shorthand for "who gets the children" under the divorce decree or judgment. In 20 states, custody is split into two types: physical custody and legal custody. Physical custody refers to the responsibility of taking care of the children, while legal custody involves making decisions that affect their interests (such as medical, educational and religious decisions). In states that don't distinguish between physical and legal custody, the term "custody" implies both types of responsibilities.

1. Does custody always go to just one parent?

No. Courts frequently award at least some aspects of custody to both parents, called "joint custody." Joint custody usually takes at least one of three forms:

- joint physical custody (children spend a relatively equal amount of time with each parent)
- joint legal custody (medical, educational, religious and other decisions about the children are shared), or
- both joint legal and joint physical custody.

In every state, courts are willing to order joint legal custody, but about half the states are reluctant to order joint physical custody unless both parents agree to it and they appear to be sufficiently able to communicate and cooperate with each other. In Idaho, New Mexico and New Hampshire, courts are required to award joint custody except where the children's best interests—or a parent's health or safety—would be compromised. Many other states expressly allow their courts to order joint custody even if one parent objects to such an arrangement.

2. Can someone other than the parents have physical or legal custody?

Sometimes neither parent can suitably assume custody of the children, perhaps because of substance abuse or a mental health problem. In these situations, others may assume temporary custody of the children under a court-ordered guardianship or foster care arrangement.

3. What factors do courts take into account when making custody and visitation decisions?

The court will normally favor the parent who will best maintain stability in the child's surroundings. There is no set standard as to what constitutes "stability," but a judge looks for continuity in a child's life. To the degree possible, a judge will try to maintain a child's school, community and religious ties.

A court gives the "best interests" of the child the highest priority. What the best interests of the child are in a given situation depends upon many factors, including:

- the child's age, gender, mental and physical health
- mental and physical health of parents
- lifestyle and other social factors of the parents, including whether the child is exposed to second-hand smoke and whether there is any history of child abuse
- the love and emotional ties between the parent and the child, as well as the parent's ability to give the child guidance
- the parent's ability to provide the child with food, shelter, clothing and medical care
- the child's established living pattern (school, home, community, religious institution)
- the quality of school—particularly important when one parent wishes to move
- the child's preference, if the child is above a certain age (usually about 12), and
- the ability and willingness of the parent to foster healthy communication and contact between the child and the other parent.

4. Are there special issues if a gay or lesbian parent is seeking custody or visitation rights?

In a few states, including Alaska, California, District of Columbia, New Mexico and Pennsylvania, a parent's sexual orientation cannot in and of itself prevent a parent from being given custody of or visitation with his or her child. As a practical matter, however, lesbian and gay parents—even in those states—may be denied custody or visitation. This is because judges, when considering the best interests of the child, may be motivated by their own or community prejudices, and may find reasons other than the lesbian or gay parent's sexual orientation to deny custody or appropriate visitation.

5. Is race ever an issue in custody or visitation decisions?

The U.S. Supreme Court has ruled it unconstitutional for a court to consider race when a noncustodial parent petitions for a change of custody. In that case, a white couple had divorced, and the mother had been awarded custody of their son. She remarried an African-American man and moved to a predominantly African-American neighborhood. The father filed a request for modification of custody based on the changed circumstance that the boy was now living with an African-American man in an African-American neighborhood. A Florida court granted the modification. The U.S. Supreme Court reversed, ruling that societal stigma, especially a racial one, cannot be the basis for a custody decision.

6. Are mothers more likely to be awarded custody over fathers?

In the past, most states provided that custody of children of "tender years" (about five and under) had to be awarded to the mother when parents divorced. This rule has been rejected in most states, or relegated to the role of tie-breaker if two fit parents request custody of their pre-school children. Only South Carolina and Tennessee continue to carry the tender years doctrine in their statutes. Most states require their courts to determine custody on the basis of what's in the children's best interests without regard to the sex of the parent.

As it turns out, most divorcing parents agree that the mother will have custody after a separation or divorce and that the father will exercise reasonable visitation. This sometimes happens because fathers presume that mothers will be awarded custody or because the mother is more tenacious in seeking custody. In still other situations, the parents agree that the mother has more time, a greater inclination or a better understanding of the children's daily needs.

7. When a court awards physical custody to one parent and "visitation at reasonable times and places" to the other, who determines what's reasonable?

The parent with physical custody is generally in the driver's seat regarding what is reasonable. This need not be bad if the parents cooperate to see that the kids spend a maximum amount of time with each parent. Unfortunately, it all too often translates into very little visitation time with the noncustodial parent, and lots of bitter disputes over missed visits and inconvenience. To avoid such problems, many courts now prefer for the parties to work out a fairly detailed parenting plan (known as a parenting agreement) which sets the visitation schedule and outlines who has responsibility for decisions affecting the children.

8. I have sole custody of my children. My ex-spouse, who lives in another state, has threatened to go to court in his state and get the custody order changed. Can he do that?

All states and the District of Columbia have enacted a statute called the Uniform Child Custody Jurisdiction Act, which sets standards for when a court may make a custody determination and when a court must defer to an existing determination from another state. Having the same law in all states helps standardize how custody decrees are treated. It also helps solve many problems created by kidnapping or disagreements over custody between parents living in different states.

In general, a state may make a custody decision about a child only if it meets one of these tests (in order of preference):

1. The state is the child's home state. This means the child has resided in the state for the six previous months, or was residing in the state but is absent because a parent took the child to another state. (A parent who wrongfully removed or retained a child in order to create a "home state" will be denied custody.)

2. The child has significant connections in the state with people such as teachers, doctors and grandparents, and, in the words of the Act, "substantial evidence in the state concerning the child's care, protection, training and personal relationships." (A parent who wrongfully removed or retained a child in order to create "significant connections" will be denied custody.)

3. The child is in the state and either has been abandoned or is in danger of being abused or neglected if sent back to the other state.

4. No other state can meet one of the above three tests, or a state that can meet at least one test has declined to make a custody decision.

If a state cannot meet one of these tests, the courts of that state cannot make a custody award, even if the child is present in the state. In the event more than one state meets the above standards, the law specifies that only one state may make custody decisions. This means that once a state makes a custody award, any other state must keep its hands off the matter.

9. I have sole physical custody of our children. Several times my ex has not returned the kids on time after taking them for a visit, and I'm scared one day he won't return them at all. What are my rights as the custodial parent?

In most states, it's a crime to take a child from his or her parent with the intent to interfere with that parent's physical custody of the child (even if the taker also has custody rights). This crime commonly is referred to as "custodial interference." In most states, the parent deprived of custody may sue the taker for damages, as well as get help from the police to have the child returned.

If a parent without physical custody (who may or may not have visitation rights) removes a child from—or refuses to return a child to—the parent with physical custody, it is considered kidnapping or child concealment in addition to custodial interference. Federal and state laws have been passed to prosecute and punish parents guilty of this type of kidnapping, which is a felony in over 40 states.

In many states, interfering with a parent's custody is a felony if the child is taken out-of-state. Many states, however, recognize good-cause defenses, such as where the taker acted to prevent imminent bodily harm to herself or himself, or to the child. In addition, some states let a parent take a child out-of-state if the parent is requesting custody in court and has notified the court or police of the child's location.

10. I've heard that mediation is the best approach to solving child custody matters. Things are so bitter between my ex and me that it's hard to see us sitting down together to work things out. How can mediation possibly work?

Mediation is a nonadversarial process where a neutral person (a mediator) meets with disputing persons to help them settle the dispute. The mediator does not, however, have power to impose a solution on the parties.

Mediation is often used to help a divorcing or divorced couple work out their differences, especially over custody and visitation disputes. Some lawyers and mental health professionals employ mediation as part of their practice. Several states require mediation in custody and visitation disputes and a number of others allow courts to order mediation. In California and a few other states, if the parties do not reach agreement, the mediator is usually asked by the court to make a recommendation. In most states, however, the mediator plays no further role if the parties can't agree.

Mediators are very skilled at getting parents who are bitter enemies to cooperate for the sake of their children. The more parents can agree on the details of separate parenting, the better it will be for them and their children. And mediators are skilled at getting the parents to recognize this fact and then move forward towards negotiating a sensible parenting agreement. If there is a history of abuse or the parents initially cannot stand to be in the same room with each other, the mediator can meet with each parent separately and ferry messages back and forth until agreement on at least some issues is reached. At this point, the parties may be willing to meet face to face.

11. Under what circumstances can custody orders be changed within the state where they were obtained?

After a final decree of divorce is filed with a court, former spouses may agree to modify the custody or visitation terms. This modified agreement (also called a "stipulated modification") may be made without court approval. If one person, however, later reneges on the agreement, the other person may not be able to enforce it unless the court has approved the modification. Thus, it is generally advisable to obtain court approval before relying on such agreements. Courts usually approve modification agreements unless it appears that they are not in the best interests of the child.

If a parent wants to change an existing court order affecting custody or visitation and the other parent won't agree to the change, he or she must file a motion requesting a modification of the order from the court that issued it, usually on the ground of changed circumstances. Requiring a showing of changed circumstances encourages stability of arrangements and helps prevent the court from becoming overburdened with frequent and repetitive modification requests. Some examples of changed circumstances:

- **Geographic move.** If a custodial parent geographically relocates a substantial distance, the move may constitute a changed circumstance that justifies the court's modification of a custody or visitation order to accommodate the needs of the noncustodial parent. Some courts switch custody from one parent to the other, although the more common approach is to ask the parents to work out a plan under which both parents may continue to have significant contacts with their children.

- **Change in lifestyle.** Changes in custody or visitation orders may be obtained if substantial changes in a parent's lifestyle threatens or harms the child. If, for example, a custodial parent begins working at night and leaving a nine year old child alone, the other parent may request a change in custody. Similarly, if a noncustodial parent begins drinking heavily or taking drugs, the custodial parent may file a request for modification of the visitation order (asking, for example, that visits occur when the parent is sober, or in the presence of another adult). What constitutes a lifestyle sufficiently detrimental to warrant a change in custody or visitation rights varies tremendously depending on the state and the particular judge deciding the case. For instance, cohabitation by a parent may be ignored in one place, but not another.

For More Help

Child Custody: Building Agreements That Work, by Mimi Lyster (Nolo Press), shows separating or divorcing parents how to build win-win custody arrangements.

Nolo's Pocket Guide to Family Law, by Robin Leonard and Stephen Elias (Nolo Press), explains legal concepts you may run across if you're involved in a divorce, custody dispute, adoption or other family law matter.

The National Center for Lesbian Rights, 870 Market St., Suite 570, San Francisco, CA 94102, 415-392-6257, provides legal information, referrals and assistance to lesbian and gay parents.

22. CHILD SUPPORT

Child support is an emotional subject. Parents who are supposed to receive it on behalf of their children often do not. Parents who are supposed to pay it often cannot, or choose not to for a variety of reasons that are not legally recognized. It is the children who suffer the most when child support levels are inadequate or obligations are not met. Therefore, the trend in all states is to increase child support levels and the ways child support obligations can be enforced.

1. How long must parents support their children?

Biological parents and adoptive parents must support their children until:

- the children reach the age of majority (and sometimes longer if the children have special needs)
- the children go on active military duty, or
- the parents' rights and responsibilities are terminated (such as when a child is adopted).

Parents are not required to support children who have been declared emancipated by a court. Emancipation can occur when a minor has demonstrated freedom from parental control or support and an ability to be self-supporting.

2. How are child support obligations affected by a divorce?

When one parent is awarded sole custody in a divorce, the other parent typically is required to fulfill his or her child support obligation by making payments to the custodial parent. The custodial parent, however, meets his or her support obligation through the custody itself. When parents are awarded joint physical custody in a divorce, the support obligation of each is often based on the ratio of each parent's income to their combined incomes, and the percentage of time the child spends with each parent.

3. Are fathers who never married the mother still required to pay child support?

The short answer to this question is yes. When a mother is not married, however, it's not always clear who the father is. An "acknowledged father" is any biological father of a child born to unmarried parents for whom paternity has been established by either the admission of the father or the agreement of the parents. Acknowledged fathers are required to pay child support.

Additionally, a man who never married may be presumed to be the father of a child if he welcomes the child into his home and openly holds the child out as his own. In some states, the presumption of paternity is considered conclusive, which means it cannot be disproved, even with contradictory blood tests.

4. Do unmarried fathers have to pay child support even if none has been ordered by a court?

Yes. The obligation to pay child support does not depend on marriage or a court order. Where most unmarried fathers encounter this principle is when the mother seeks public assistance. Sooner or later the welfare department will pursue the father for reimbursement based on his support obligation. Sometimes this happens many years later, and the father is required to pay thousands of dollars in back support that he never knew he owed because there was no court order.

5. Is a stepfather obligated to support the children of the woman to whom he is married?

No, unless he legally adopts the children.

6. What factors are used to calculate child support?

Under the federal Child Support Enforcement Act of 1984, each state must develop guidelines to calculate a range of child support to be paid, based on the parents' incomes and expenses. These guidelines vary considerably from state to state, which means that in virtually identical situations the child support ordered in one state may be far more or less than that ordered in another state. Most states allow their judges considerable leeway in setting the actual amount, as long as the general state guidelines are followed. A few states, including California, do not trust their judges to be consistent and therefore impose very strict guidelines that leave the judges very little latitude.

Regardless of how much latitude judges are given, the guidelines in effect in most states specify factors which must be considered in determining who pays child support, and how much. These factors usually include:

- the needs of the child—including health insurance, educational needs, day care and special needs
- the needs of the custodial parent
- the paying parent's ability to pay, and
- the standard of living of the child before divorce.

7. Can my child support payments be based on my ability to earn rather than on my actual income?

In most states, the judge is authorized to examine a parent's ability to earn as well as what he or she is actually earning, and order higher child support if there is a discrepancy. Actual earnings are an important factor in determining a person's ability to earn, but are not conclusive where there is evidence that a person could earn more if she chose to do so. For example, assume a parent with an obligation to pay child support leaves his current job and enrolls in medical or law school, takes a job with lower pay but good potential for higher pay in the future, or takes a lower paying job that provides better job satisfaction. In each of these situations, a court may base the child support award on the income from the original job (ability to earn) rather than on the new income level (ability to pay). The basis for this decision would be that the children's current needs take priority over the parent's career plans and desires.

8. What happens I fall behind on my child support payments?

Each installment of court-ordered child support is to be paid according to the date set out in the order. When a person does not comply with the order, the overdue payments are called arrearages or arrears. Judges have become very strict about enforcing child support orders and collecting arrearages. While the person with arrears can ask a judge for a downward modification of future payments, the judge will usually insist that the arrearage be paid in full, either immediately or in installments. In fact, judges in most states are prohibited by law from retroactively modifying a child support obligation. Assume, for example, that Joe has a child support obligation of $300 per month. Joe is laid off of his job, and six months pass before he finds another one with comparable pay. Although Joe could seek a temporary decrease on the grounds of diminished income, he lets the matter slide and fails to pay any support during the six-month period. Joe's ex-wife later brings Joe into court to collect the $1,800 arrearage; Joe cannot obtain a retroactive ruling excusing him from making the earlier payments.

9. My ex-spouse is refusing to pay court ordered child support. How can I see to it that the order is enforced?

Under the Child Support Enforcement Act of 1984, the district attorneys (or state's attorneys) of every state must help you collect the child support owed by your ex. Sometimes this means that the D.A. will serve your ex with papers requiring him to meet with the D.A. and arrange a payment schedule, and telling him that if he refuses to meet or pay, he could go to jail. If your ex has moved out of state, you or the D.A. can use legal procedures to locate him and seek payment. Federal and state parent locator services can also assist in locating missing parents.

Federal laws permit the interception of tax refunds to enforce child support orders. Other methods of enforcement include wage attachments, seizing property, suspending the business license of a payer who is behind on child support or—in some states—going after the payer's driver's license. Your state's D.A. may employ any one of these methods in an attempt to help you collect from your ex.

If you and your ex live in different states, you may use the Revised Uniform Reciprocal Enforcement of Support Act (RURESA) to seek payment. Under that law, the court in the state where you live contacts a court in your ex-spouse's state, which in turn requires him to pay. This procedure will be provided to you free of charge. Unfortunately, however, it often falls short of its stated goals due to the complexity of the process and the low priority frequently assigned to these cases by the courts and law enforcement officers which are involved.

As a last resort, the court that has issued the child support order can hold your ex in contempt and, in the absence of a reasonable explanation for the delinquency, impose a jail term. This contempt power is exercised sparingly in most states, primarily because most judges would rather keep the payer out of jail where he has a chance of earning the income necessary to pay the support.

10. I think our existing child support order is unfair. How can I change it?

You and your former spouse may agree to modify the child support terms, but even an agreed-upon modification for child support must be approved by a judge to be legally enforceable.

If you and your ex can't agree on a change, you must request the court to hold a hearing in which each of you can argue the pros and cons of the proposed modification. As a general rule, the court will not modify an existing order unless the parent proposing the modification can show changed circumstances. This rule encourages stability of arrangements and helps prevent the court from becoming overburdened with frequent and repetitive modification requests.

Depending on the circumstances, a modification may be temporary or permanent. Examples of the types of changes that frequently support temporary modification orders are:

- a child's medical emergency
- the payer's temporary inability to pay (for instance, because of illness or an additional financial burden such as a medical emergency or job loss), or
- temporary economic or medical hardship on the part of the parent to whom child support is owed.

A permanent modification may be awarded under one of the following circumstances:

- either parent receives additional income from remarriage
- changes in the child support laws
- job change of either parent
- cost of living increase
- disability of either parent, or
- needs of the child.

A permanent modification of a child support order will remain in effect until support is no longer required or the order is modified again at a later time.

11. Do I have to pay child support if my ex keeps me away from my kids?

Yes. Child support should not be confused with custody and visitation. Every parent has an obligation to support his or her children. With one narrow exception, no state allows a parent to withhold support because of disputes over visitation. The exception? If the custodial parent disappears for a lengthy period so that no visitation is possible, a few courts have ruled that the noncustodial parent's duty to pay child support may be considered temporarily suspended.

No matter what the circumstances, if you believe that your visitation rights are being interfered with, the appropriate remedy is to go back to court to have your rights enforced rather than stop making support payments.

For More Help

How to Raise or Lower Child Support in California, by Roderic Duncan and Warren Siegel (Nolo Press), contains forms and instructions for going to court to get an existing order changed to the appropriate level.

Nolo's Pocket Guide to Family Law, by Robin Leonard and Stephen Elias (Nolo Press), explains legal concepts you may run across if you're involved in a divorce, custody dispute, adoption or other family law matter.

23. Living Together— Gay and Straight

Many laws are designed to govern and protect the property ownership rights of married couples. But no such laws exist for unmarried couples. If you and your partner are unmarried, you must take steps to protect your relationship and define your property rights. You may also face unique problems concerning your children.

1. My partner and I don't own much property. Do we really have to make a written contract covering who owns what?

If you haven't been together long and don't own much, it's really not necessary. But the longer you live together, the more important it is to prepare a written contract making it clear who owns what—especially if you begin to accumulate a lot of property. Otherwise, you might face a serious (and potentially expensive) battle if you split up and can't agree on how to divide your property. And when things are good, taking the time to draft a well-thought out contract helps you clarify your intentions.

2. My partner makes a lot more money than I do. Should our property agreements cover who is entitled to her income and the items we purchase with it?

Absolutely. Although each person starts out owning all of his or her job-related income, many states allow this to be changed by an oral contract or even by a contract implied from the circumstances of how you live. These types of contracts are ripe for misunderstanding. For example, absent a written agreement stating whether income will be shared or kept separate, one partner might falsely claim the other promised to split their income 50–50. Although this can be tough to prove in court, the very fact that a lawsuit can be brought creates a huge problem. For obvious reasons, it's an especially a good idea to make a written agreement if a person with a big income is living with and supporting someone with little or no income.

3. What is palimony? And should we make any agreements about it?

Palimony is a phrase coined by journalists—not a legal concept—to describe the division of property or alimony-like support given by one partner in an unmarried couple by the other after a break up. Members of unmarried couples are not legally entitled to such payments unless there has been an agreement. Again, to avoid any cries for palimony, it's best to include in a written agreement whether or not one person will make payments to the other.

4. Is it essential to write something down if we buy a house together?

Yes, and it's best to cover at least four major subject areas:

- How much does each person own? If it's not 50–50, state whether there is a way for the person who owns less than half to increase his share later—for example, by fixing up the house or making a larger share of the mortgage payment.
- How is title (ownership) to be listed on the deed? One choice is as "joint tenants with rights of survivorship," meaning that when one partner dies, the other automatically inherits the whole house. Another option is "tenants in common," meaning that when one partner dies, that share of the house goes to whoever is named in a will or trust, or goes to blood relatives if the deceased partner left no estate plan.
- What happens to the house if the couple breaks up? Will one partner have the first right to stay in the house (perhaps because he or she has a young child) and buy the other out, or will the house be sold and the proceeds divided?
- If one partner has a buyout right, how will the house be appraised and how long will the buyout take?

5. My partner and I have a young son, and I'm thinking of giving up my job to stay home and care for him full-time. If my partner and I ever split up, can I be compensated for my loss of income?

This is a personal—not a legal—decision. If you and your partner decide that compensation is fair, there are many ways to arrange it. For example, you could make an agreement stating that if you break up while you're still providing childcare, your partner will pay an agreed-upon amount to help you make the transition. Or, you might agree in writing that your partner will pay you a salary during the time you stay at home, including Social Security and other required benefits.

6. Am I liable for the debts of my partner?

Not unless you have specifically undertaken responsibility to pay a particular debt—for example, as a cosigner or if the debt is charged to a joint account. By contrast, husbands and wives are generally liable for all debts incurred during marriage, even those incurred by the other person. The one exception for unmarried couples applies if you have registered as domestic partners in a city where the domestic partner ordinance states that you agree to pay for each other's "basic living expenses" (food, shelter and clothing).

7. If one of us dies, how much property will the survivor inherit?

Nothing, unless the deceased partner made a will or used another estate planning device such as a living trust or joint tenancy agreement, or, if under the terms of a contract (such as to jointly buy a house), the survivor already owns part of the property. This is unlike the legal situation married couples enjoy, where in the absence of a will, a surviving spouse automatically inherits a major portion of a deceased spouse's property under "intestate succession" laws. The bottom line is simple: To protect the person you live with, it's essential that you specifically leave him or her property using a will, living trust or other legal document.

8. If I am injured or incapacitated, can my partner make medical or financial decisions on my behalf?

Not unless you have executed a document called a "durable power of attorney" giving your partner the specific authority to make those decisions (see Chapter 18. Durable Power of Attorney for Finances and Chapter 19. Healthcare Directives). You and your partner should each do this unless you really don't care who will handle the finances and make the necessary medical decisions when one of you can't. Without a durable power of attorney, huge emotional and practical problems can result. For example, the fate of a severely ill or injured person could be in the hands of a biological relative who disapproves of his or her relationship and who makes medical decisions contrary to what he or she wants. It is far better to prepare the necessary paperwork so the loving and knowing partner will be the primary decision-maker.

9. Do unmarried couples face any special parenting concerns?

Yes, several:

- Straight couples who have children together need to take steps to ensure that both are recognized as the legal parents. Both parents should be listed on the birth certificate, and at a minimum the father should sign a statement of paternity. Even better, both parents should sign a statement of parentage acknowledging the father's paternity.

- All unmarried couples—straight and gay—face potential obstacles in adopting together. All states favor married couples as adoptive parents. Two states (New Hampshire and Florida) expressly prohibit lesbians and gay men from adopting. This doesn't mean the other states welcome same-sex couples or that any state reaches out to help straight unmarried couples adopt. In fact, all unmarried couples must work extra hard with local social workers to obtain favorable recommendations. During the past ten years or so, unmarried (mostly lesbian and gay, but some straight) couples have been granted adoptions in over a dozen states. Many of those states have also granted "second parent" adoptions to the partner of the biological parent, without the biological parent's rights being terminated.

- Members of unmarried couples who have children from former marriages face the potential prejudice of an ex-spouse or a judge called on to make a custody determination. In most states, this is a much greater concern for lesbian and gay parents than for straight ones, as judges (with the exception of a few states which also come down hard on any unmarried couple) tend to be more tolerant of opposite-sex cohabitation than same-sex cohabitation. Many judges prefer to place children with a heterosexual, married parent, if that's an option.

10. If my partner and I live together long enough, won't we have a common law marriage?

Not necessarily. A common law marriage can occur only when:

- a straight couple (no same-sex couple can have a common law marriage) lives together in Alabama, Colorado, Georgia, Idaho, Iowa, Kansas,

    Montana, Oklahoma, Pennsylvania, Rhode Island, South Carolina, Texas, Utah or Washington, DC

- for a significant period of time (it is not defined in any state)
- holding themselves out as a married couple (typically using the same last name, referring to the other as "my husband" or "my wife" and filing a joint tax return), and
- intending to be married.

Unless all four of those things are true, there is no common law marriage. When one exists, the couple must go through a formal divorce to end the relationship.

For More Help

The Living Together Kit, by Ralph Warner and Toni Ihara (Nolo Press), explains the legal rules that apply to unmarried couples and includes sample contracts governing jointly-owned property.

A Legal Guide for Lesbian and Gay Couples, by Hayden Curry, Denis Clifford and Robin Leonard (Nolo Press), sets out the law and contains sample agreements for same-sex couples.

24. Small Claims Court

Small claims court judges resolve disputes involving relatively modest amounts of money. The people involved present their case to a judge or court commissioner under rules that encourage a minimum of legal and procedural formality. The judge in turn makes a decision (a judgment) reasonably promptly. Although procedural rules dealing with when and where to file and serve papers are established by each state's laws and differ in detail, the basic approach to properly preparing and presenting a small claims case is remarkably similar everywhere.

1. How much can I sue for in small claims court?

The limit is normally between $2,000 and $7,500, depending on the state in which you file. For instance, the maximum is $3,000 in New York, $5,000 in California, $7,500 in Minnesota and $2,500 in Washington.

2. Can any kind of case be resolved in small claims court?

No. Small claims courts primarily resolve small monetary disputes. In a few states, however, small claims courts may also rule on a limited range of other types of legal disputes, such as evictions or requests for the return of an item of property (restitution). You cannot use small claims court to file a divorce, guardianship, name change or bankruptcy, or to ask for emergency relief (such as an injunction to stop someone from doing an illegal act).

When it comes to disputes involving money, you can usually file in small claims court based on any legal theory that would be allowed in any other court—for example, breach of contract, personal injury, intentional harm or breach of warranty. A few states do, however, limit or prohibit small claims suits based on libel, slander or false arrest.

Finally, suits against the federal government, a federal agency or even against a federal employee for actions relating to his or her employment should not be brought in small claims court. Suits against the federal government normally must be filed in federal District Court. Unfortunately, there are no federal small claims procedures available except in federal Tax Court.

3. Is there a way to get my money without suing?

Even if you've been turned down by phone or in person (maybe even including a nasty argument), try asking for your money at least once more. This time, make your demand in the form of a straightforward letter, concluding with the statement that you'll file in small claims court in ten days unless payment is received. Unlike a conversation, where the other party may assume you'll never follow up, a demand letter is like a slap in the face that lets the person know you're serious about getting paid. Because many individuals and small business people have a strong aversion to the idea of a public trial (including the time and trouble it takes), making it clear you are prepared to file a lawsuit can be an effective catalyst to getting the other party to talk settlement.

In addition, many states offer, and a few require, a community- or court-based mediation program designed to help the parties arrive at their own compromise settlement with the help of a neutral third party. Mediation works best where the parties have an interest in staying on good terms, as is generally the case with neighbors, family members or small business people who have done business together for many years. But because mediation doesn't always end up with the parties agreeing, it's still often necessary to present the case in small claims court.

4. Are there time limits in which a small claims court case must be filed?

Yes. States establish rules called "statutes of limitation," which dictate how long you may wait to initiate a lawsuit after the key event giving rise to the lawsuit occurs or, in some instances, is discovered. Statutes of limitation rules apply to all courts, including small claims.

You'll almost always have at least one year to sue (measured from the event). Often, you'll have much longer. For example, in many states, the statute of limitations period is two years for the breach of an oral contract and four years when a written contract is broken. If you're planning to sue a state or local government agency, however, such as a city or county, you'll often need to file a formal claim with that agency within three to six months of the incident. Only after your initial timely complaint is denied are you eligible to file in small claims court.

As a practical matter, you'll always want to sue promptly, so that memories are fresh. If you do, there is usually no need to worry about limitations periods. If some time has already passed since the incident occurred—for example, after the breach of a written contract or a personal injury—you may need to do a little research to determine whether you can still file your claim. Check your state's legal code under the index heading "statute of limitation."

5. Where should I file my small claims lawsuit?

Assuming the other party lives or does business in your state, you'll usually sue in the small claims district closest to their residence or headquarters. In some instances, you may need to sue in the district where a contract was signed or a personal injury occurred (such as an auto accident). Check with your small claims clerk for detailed rules.

If a defendant has no contact with your state, you'll generally have to sue in the state where the defendant lives or operates. Because of the distance involved, out-of-state small claims lawsuits tend to be expensive and unwieldy.

6. Am I guaranteed payment if I win the lawsuit?

Unfortunately, the answer is no. The court may decide that you win the lawsuit, but it won't handle collection for you. So before you sue, always ask, "Can I collect if I win?" If not, think twice before suing.

Worrying about whether or not you can get paid is reasonable, because some people and businesses are "judgment proof"—that is, they have no money or assets and aren't likely to acquire any in the foreseeable future. If you are suing an individual, ask yourself whether the person has a steady job, valuable real property or investments. If yes, it should be reasonably easy to collect if you win. If no, try to identify another collection source, such as a bank account, before going forward. It's also wise to consider whether this person may be more solvent in the future, as court judgments are good for at least 20 years in many states and can usually be renewed for a longer period. While a person may have no assets now, he or she could inherit money, win the lottery, get a good job or otherwise have an economic turn-around sometime down the road.

7. If I'm sued in small claims court, but the other party is really at fault, can I countersue?

In most states, you can countersue as long as your claim arises out of the same event or transaction. Usually, if the amount you sue for is under the small claims limit, your case will remain in that court. If, however, you want to sue for more, check with your small claims clerk for applicable rules. Often, you'll need to have the case transferred to a different court which has the power to handle cases where more money is at stake.

8. Can I hire a lawyer to represent me in small claims court?

In a minority of states, including California, Nebraska and Michigan, the answer is no. In most states, however, you can be represented by a lawyer. But even where it's allowed, hiring a lawyer is rarely cost-efficient, given the high prices attorneys charge compared to the relatively small amounts of money involved in small claims disputes. Happily, several studies show that people who represent themselves in small claims cases usually do just as well as those who have a lawyer.

9. What should I do to prepare my small claims case?

Whether you are a plaintiff (the person suing) or the defendant (person being sued), the key is to realize that it's usually what you bring with you to court to back up your story—not what you say—that determines whether you'll win or lose. This makes sense if you understand that the judge has no idea who you are and whether your oral (spoken) testimony is reliable. After all, your opponent is likely to claim that the "true story" is extremely different from your version.

In short, your chances of winning will greatly increase if you carefully collect and prepare your evidence. Depending on the type of case, a few of the tools you can use to convince the judge you are right include eye witnesses, photographs, letters from experts, advertisements hyping products or services, written leases and contracts.

10. What's the best way to present my case to a judge?

Realize that the judge is busy and has heard dozens of stories like yours. To keep the judge's attention, get to the point fast by first describing the actual event that gave rise to your claim. Immediately follow up by stating how much money you are requesting. To be able to do this efficiently, it's best to practice in advance. Here is an example of a good start: "Your Honor, my car was damaged on January 10, 1996, when the defendant ran a red light at Rose and Hyacinth Streets in the town of Saginaw and hit my front fender. I have a canceled check to show it cost me $427 to fix the fender."

After you have clearly stated the key event, double back and tell the judge the events that led up to your loss. For example, you might now explain that you were driving below the speed limit and had entered the intersection when the light was green, and you did your best to avoid the defendant's car.

11. Will witnesses need to testify in person?

If possible, it's best to have key witnesses present in court. But if this isn't convenient, a clear memo or letter will be allowed under the rules of most small claims courts. Have the witness start the statement by establishing who he or she is. ("My name is John Lomox. I've owned and managed Reo's Toyota Repair Service for the last 17 years.") In clear, unemotional language, the witness should explain what he or she observed or heard. ("I carefully checked Mary Wilson's engine and found that it has been rebuilt improperly, using worn-out parts.") Finally, the witness should try to anticipate any questions a reasonable person might ask and provide the answers. ("Although it can take a few days to get new parts for older engines, such as the one Mary Wilson owned, it is easy and common practice to do so.")

12. If I lose my case in small claims court, can I appeal?

The answer depends on the state in which you live. Many states allow either party to appeal within a certain period of time, often 30 days. In some states, appeals must be based solely on the ground that the judge made a legal mistake, and not on the facts of the case. Other states have their own unique rules. In California, for example, a defendant may appeal to the Superior Court within 30 days. A plaintiff may not appeal at all, but can make a motion to correct clerical errors or to correct a decision based on a legal mistake.

To find the law for your state, call your local Small Claims Court clerk.

For More Help

Everybody's Guide to Small Claims Court, (Nolo Press) (National and California Editions), by Ralph Warner, explains how to evaluate your case, prepare for court and convince a judge you're right.

Collect Your Court Judgment, by Gini Graham Scott, Stephen Elias and Lisa Goldoftas (Nolo Press), explains 19 ways to collect after you win a lawsuit in California.

25. Legal Malpractice

For any number of reasons, you may be mad at a lawyer you hired to do legal work for you. Perhaps your lawyer has failed to keep you informed about your case, to meet deadlines or to do what you believe is quality work. Maybe your lawyer has sent you a bill for far more than you believe is reasonable. Whatever the specifics of your situation, you're sure that something has gone wrong with your professional relationship. These questions touch on the reasons for most complaints against attorneys and offer suggestions as to what you can do about them.

1. I've lost confidence in my lawyer. Can I fire him?

Yes, you have the right to end a relationship with a lawyer at any time, but unless he's truly awful, it's often not wise to do so unless you have another lawyer lined up or plan to handle the case yourself.

2. I fired my lawyer, but I need my file. How do I get it?

Ask, or sign an authorization allowing any new attorney to get it. Even if you have a fee dispute with your former lawyer or you simply have not paid him or her, you are entitled to get your file.

3. My lawyer isn't returning my phone calls. Is this malpractice?

No. But, it's a sign of trouble. Try to find out why your lawyer is not returning your phone calls. (He or she may be busy, rude, sick or procrastinating.) As you do this, examine the possibility that your lawyer may be avoiding you for a good reason—you may be too demanding. A good way to deal with this situation is to write or fax the lawyer a straightforward letter explaining your difficulty in communicating and asking for a phone call or meeting to re-establish or restore your relationship. If this doesn't work, consider firing the lawyer and/or filing a formal complaint with your state's attorney regulatory agency.

4. My lawyer seems to have stopped working on my case. Is this malpractice?

The longer your attorney ignores you and your case, the more likely it is to amount to malpractice. You must act quickly to see that your case is properly handled and get another lawyer if necessary. Writing or faxing a letter expressing your concerns and asking for a meeting is a good first step.

5. My lawyer obviously screwed up my case. Can I sue her for malpractice?

Unfortunately, it is very hard to win a malpractice case. Malpractice simply means that the lawyer failed to use the ordinary skill and care that would be used by other lawyers in handling a similar problem or case under similar circumstances. Put more bluntly—to be liable for malpractice, your lawyer must have made a serious mistake or handled your case improperly or incompetently.

To win a malpractice case against an attorney, you must prove four basic things:

- duty—that the attorney owed you a duty to act properly
- breach—that the attorney breached the duty, was negligent, made a mistake or did not do what he or she agreed to do

- causation—that this conduct caused you damages, and
- damages—that you suffered financial losses as a result.

Causation may be your biggest hurdle. To win a malpractice case, you must prove both the malpractice action against your attorney and the underlying case that the lawyer mishandled. Then, you will have to show that if you would have won the underlying case, you would have been able to collect from the defendant. For example, say you were hit by a car when you were walking across the street, and you hired a lawyer who didn't file the lawsuit on time. You sue for malpractice and can easily prove the driver's liability. To win the malpractice case against your lawyer, however, you'd also have to show that the driver had money or insurance. If you can't show that the driver had assets which could have been used to pay the judgment, you won't win your malpractice case, even though the lawyer clearly blew it and the driver was clearly at fault.

6. My case was thrown out of court because my lawyer did no work. Is this grounds to sue my lawyer?

Maybe. Your lawyer is responsible for whatever money you could have won had the case been properly handled. Your difficulty will be in proving not only that your lawyer mishandled the case, but that if handled correctly, you could have won and collected a judgment.

7. My lawyer originally said my case was worth six figures and then later insisted that I settle for peanuts—can I sue the lawyer for the difference?

No. Your lawyer may have given you an inflated estimate of the value of your case to encourage you to hire her. Get your file from your lawyer and get a second opinion on your case. If another reputable lawyer believes you are being advised to settle for too little, consider changing lawyers.

8. Can I sue my lawyer for settling my case without my authorization?

Yes, but you would have to prove that the settlement your lawyer entered into was for less than your case was worth.

9. I saw my lawyer playing tennis with the opposing lawyer— is this a breach of attorney ethics?

No. There is nothing ethically wrong with opposing attorneys playing tennis, bridge, golf or enjoying other common social interactions. If they talk about your case (on the tennis court or anywhere else), however, and your lawyer lets slip something that you said in confidence, that would be a clear violation of your attorney's duty to you.

Even though socializing with the opposing counsel isn't a violation of ethical rules, in the real world it can obviously make a big difference how you found out about it. If your lawyer told you he occasionally played tennis with the opposing attorney when you first discussed your case, you clearly had a chance to hire another lawyer if it bothered you. But what if you head to the tennis court for a game after being grilled by the opposing attorney at your deposition, only to run into your lawyer playing with the legal barracuda who just tried to eat you for lunch? It would have been wise for your attorney to tell you about his social relationship with the other lawyer when you first met. Although in failing to do this your attorney hasn't breached any ethical duty to you, you may wish to change attorneys.

10. My lawyer sent me a huge and unexpected bill. What can I do about it?

Don't pay it right away. Ask to discuss your concerns with the lawyer. If you're not satisfied with your lawyer's explanation, ask for a reduction of the bill. If the lawyer refuses, consider filing for nonbinding fee arbitration with a state or local bar association. Arbitration is a process where a neutral decisionmaker resolves your fee dispute. "Nonbinding" means you are free to reject the arbitrator's decision. Get the rules from your state or local bar association before you agree to arbitration. If the arbitration is to be conducted by lawyers who may be biased against you, don't agree to a binding result—meaning a result you aren't allowed to reject.

11. I'm worried that my lawyer may have misappropriated some of the money I paid as a retainer. What should I do?

If you seriously suspect your lawyer has misused any money he holds for you in trust, complain to your state's attorney regulatory agency pronto. Although regulation of lawyers is lax in most states, complaints about stealing clients' money are almost always taken seriously and acted on promptly. A few states have funds to reimburse clients when lawyers are caught stealing.

For More Help

Mad at Your Lawyer, by Tanya Starnes (Nolo Press), explains how to handle problems with your lawyer, from poor communication and high bills to stealing your money.

BUSINESS

Business Plans to Game Plans	1st	$29.95	GAME
Helping Employees Achieve Retirement Security	1st	$16.95	HEAR
 Hiring Indepedent Contractors: The Employer's Legal Guide	1st	$29.95	HICI
How to Finance a Growing Business	4th	$24.95	GROW
How to Form a CA Nonprofit Corp.—w/Corp. Records Binder & PC Disk	1st	$49.95	CNP
How to Form a Nonprofit Corp., Book w/Disk (PC)—National Edition	3rd	$39.95	NNP
How to Form Your Own Calif. Corp.—w/Corp. Records Binder & PC Disk	1st	$39.95	CACI
How to Form Your Own California Corporation	8th	$29.95	CCOR
How to Form Your Own Florida Corporation, (Book w/Disk—PC)	3rd	$39.95	FLCO
How to Form Your Own New York Corporation, (Book w/Disk—PC)	3rd	$39.95	NYCO
How to Form Your Own Texas Corporation, (Book w/Disk—PC)	4th	$39.95	TCI
How to Handle Your Workers' Compensation Claim (California Edition)	1st	$29.95	WORK
How to Market a Product for Under $500	1st	$29.95	UN500
How to Write a Business Plan	4th	$21.95	SBS
Make Up Your Mind: Entrepreneurs Talk About Decision Making	1st	$19.95	MIND
Managing Generation X: How to Bring Out the Best in Young Talent	1st	$19.95	MANX
Marketing Without Advertising	1st	$14.00	MWAD
Mastering Diversity: Managing for Success Under ADA and Other Anti-Discrimination Laws	1st	$29.95	MAST
OSHA in the Real World: (Book w/Disk—PC)	1st	$29.95	OSHA
Taking Care of Your Corporation, Vol. 1, (Book w/Disk—PC)	1st	$26.95	CORK
Taking Care of Your Corporation, Vol. 2, (Book w/Disk—PC)	1st	$39.95	CORK2
Tax Savvy for Small Business	1st	$26.95	SAVVY
The California Nonprofit Corporation Handbook	7th	$29.95	NON
The California Professional Corporation Handbook	5th	$34.95	PROF
The Employer's Legal Handbook	1st	$29.95	EMPL

Book on disk

TO ORDER CALL 800-992-6656

The Independent Paralegal's Handbook	3rd	$29.95	PARA
The Legal Guide for Starting & Running a Small Business	2nd	$24.95	RUNS
The Partnership Book: How to Write a Partnership Agreement	4th	$24.95	PART
Rightful Termination	1st	$29.95	RITE
Sexual Harassment on the Job	2nd	$18.95	HARS
Trademark: How to Name Your Business & Product	2nd	$29.95	TRD
Workers' Comp for Employers	2nd	$29.95	CNTRL
Your Rights in the Workplace	2nd	$15.95	YRW

CONSUMER

Fed Up With the Legal System: What's Wrong & How to Fix It	2nd	$9.95	LEG
Glossary of Insurance Terms	5th	$14.95	GLINT
How to Insure Your Car	1st	$12.95	INCAR
How to Win Your Personal Injury Claim	1st	$24.95	PICL
Nolo's Pocket Guide to California Law	4th	$10.95	CLAW
Nolo's Pocket Guide to Consumer Rights	2nd	$12.95	CAG
The Over 50 Insurance Survival Guide	1st	$16.95	OVER50
True Odds: How Risk Affects Your Everyday Life	1st	$19.95	TROD
What Do You Mean It's Not Covered?	1st	$19.95	COVER

ESTATE PLANNING & PROBATE

How to Probate an Estate (California Edition)	8th	$34.95	PAE
Make Your Own Living Trust	2nd	$19.95	LITR
Nolo's Simple Will Book	2nd	$17.95	SWIL
Plan Your Estate	3rd	$24.95	NEST
The Quick and Legal Will Book	1st	$15.95	QUIC
Nolo's Law Form Kit: Wills	1st	$14.95	KWL

FAMILY MATTERS

A Legal Guide for Lesbian and Gay Couples	8th	$24.95	LG
Child Custody: Building Agreements That Work	1st	$24.95	CUST
Divorce & Money: How to Make the Best Financial Decisions During Divorce	2nd	$21.95	DIMO

⌨ Book on disk

TO ORDER CALL 800-992-6656

How to Adopt Your Stepchild in California	4th	$22.95	ADOP
How to Do Your Own Divorce in California	21st	$24.95	CDIV
How to Do Your Own Divorce in Texas	6th	$19.95	TDIV
How to Raise or Lower Child Support in California	3rd	$18.95	CHLD
Nolo's Pocket Guide to Family Law	4th	$14.95	FLD
Practical Divorce Solutions	1st	$14.95	PDS
The Guardianship Book (California Edition)	2nd	$24.95	GB
The Living Together Kit	7th	$24.95	LTK

GOING TO COURT

Collect Your Court Judgment (California Edition)	2nd	$19.95	JUDG
Everybody's Guide to Municipal Court (California Edition)	1st	$29.95	MUNI
Everybody's Guide to Small Claims Court (California Edition)	12th	$18.95	CSCC
Everybody's Guide to Small Claims Court (National Edition)	6th	$18.95	NSCC
Fight Your Ticket ... and Win! (California Edition)	6th	$19.95	FYT
How to Change Your Name (California Edition)	6th	$24.95	NAME
Represent Yourself in Court: How to Prepare & Try a Winning Case	1st	$29.95	RYC
The Criminal Records Book (California Edition)	5th	$21.95	CRIM

HOMEOWNERS, LANDLORDS & TENANTS

	Dog Law	2nd	$12.95	DOG
💾	Every Landlord's Legal Guide (National Edition)	1st	$29.95	ELLI
	For Sale by Owner (California Edition)	2nd	$24.95	FSBO
	Homestead Your House (California Edition)	8th	$9.95	HOME
	How to Buy a House in California	3rd	$24.95	BHCA
	Neighbor Law: Fences, Trees, Boundaries & Noise	2nd	$16.95	NEI
	Safe Homes, Safe Neighborhoods: Stopping Crime Where You Live	1st	$14.95	SAFE
	Tenants' Rights (California Edition)	12th	$18.95	CTEN
	The Deeds Book (California Edition)	3rd	$16.95	DEED
	The Landlord's Law Book, Vol. 1: Rights & Responsibilities (Calif. Ed.)	5th	$34.95	LBRT
	The Landlord's Law Book, Vol. 2: Evictions (California Edition)	5th	$34.95	LBEV

💾 Book on disk

HUMOR

29 Reasons Not to Go to Law School	1st	$9.95	29R
Poetic Justice	1st	$9.95	PJ

IMMIGRATION

How to Become a United States Citizen	5th	$14.95	CIT
How to Get a Green Card: Legal Ways to Stay in the U.S.A.	2nd	$24.95	GRN
U.S. Immigration Made Easy	5th	$39.95	IMEZ

MONEY MATTERS

Building Your Nest Egg With Your 401(k)	1st	$16.95	EGG
Chapter 13 Bankruptcy: Repay Your Debts	1st	$29.95	CH13
How to File for Bankruptcy	5th	$25.95	HFB
Money Troubles: Legal Strategies to Cope With Your Debts	3rd	$18.95	MT
Nolo's Law Form Kit: Personal Bankruptcy	1st	$14.95	KBNK
Nolo's Law Form Kit: Rebuild Your Credit	1st	$14.95	KCRD
Simple Contracts for Personal Use	2nd	$16.95	CONT
Smart Ways to Save Money During and After Divorce	1st	$14.95	SAVMO
Stand Up to the IRS	2nd	$21.95	SIRS

PATENTS AND COPYRIGHTS

Copyright Your Software	1st	$39.95	CYS
Patent, Copyright & Trademark:			
A Desk Reference to Intellectual Property Law	1st	$24.95	PCTM
Patent It Yourself	4th	$39.95	PAT
🖳 Software Development: A Legal Guide (Book with disk—PC)	1st	$44.95	SFT
The Copyright Handbook: How to Protect and Use Written Works	2nd	$24.95	COHA
The Inventor's Notebook	1st	$19.95	INOT

RESEARCH & REFERENCE

Law on the Net	1st	$39.95	LAWN
Legal Research: How to Find & Understand the Law	4th	$19.95	LRES
Legal Research Made Easy (Video)	1st	$89.95	LRME

🖳 Book on disk

SENIORS

Beat the Nursing Home Trap: A Consumer's Guide	2nd	$18.95	ELD
Social Security, Medicare & Pensions	6th	$19.95	SOA
The Conservatorship Book (California Edition)	2nd	$29.95	CNSV

SOFTWARE

California Incorporator 2.0—DOS	2.0	$47.97	INCI2
Living Trust Maker 2.0—Macintosh	2.0	$47.97	LTM2
Living Trust Maker 2.0—Windows	2.0	$47.97	LTWI2
Small Business Legal Pro—Macintosh	2.0	$39.95	SBM2
Small Business Legal Pro—Windows	2.0	$39.95	SBW2
Nolo's Partnership Maker 1.0—DOS	1.0	$47.97	PAGI1
Nolo's Personal RecordKeeper 3.0—Macintosh	3.0	$29.97	FRM3
Patent It Yourself 1.0—Windows	1.0	$149.97	PYW1
WillMaker 6.0—Macintosh	6.0	$41.97	WM6
WillMaker 6.0—Windows	6.0	$41.97	WIW6

SPECIAL UPGRADE OFFER

Get 25% off the latest edition of your Nolo book

It's important to have the most current legal information. Because laws and legal procedures change often, we update our books regularly. To help keep you up-to-date we are extending this special upgrade offer. Cut out and mail the title portion of the cover of your old Nolo book and we'll give you 25% off the retail price of the NEW EDITION when you purchase directly from us. For more information call us at 1-800-992-6656. This offer is to individuals only.

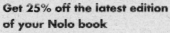
 Book on disk

ORDER FORM

Code	Quantity	Title	Unit price	Total
			Subtotal	
		In California add appropriate Sales Tax		

Shipping & Handling ($5 for 1st item; $6 for 2-3 items, 7$ for 4 or more)

UPS RUSH delivery $7-any size order*

TOTAL

Name

Address

UPS to street address, Priority Mail to P.O. boxes

* Delivered in 3 business days from receipt of order. S.F. Bay area use regular shipping.

FOR FASTER SERVICE, USE YOUR CREDIT CARD & OUR TOLL-FREE NUMBERS

ORDER 24 HOURS A DAY	1-800-992-6656
FAX US YOUR ORDER	1-800-645-0895
e-MAIL	cs@nolo.com
GENERAL INFORMATION	1-800-549-1976
CUSTOMER SERVICE	1-800-728-3555, Mon.-Sat. 9am-5pm, PST

METHOD OF PAYMENT

☐ Check enclosed

☐ VISA ☐ MasterCard ☐ Discover Card ☐ American Express

Account #   Expiration Date

Authorizing Signature

Daytime Phone

Send to: Nolo Press, 950 Parker Street, Berkeley, CA 94710

PRICES SUBJECT TO CHANGE

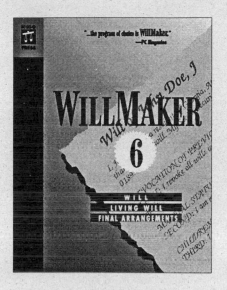

FREE SUBSCRIPTION
WITH ANY PURCHASE

Purchase any product from Nolo Press and get a free, two-year subscription to the Nolo *News*. We'll start (or extend) your subscription automatically. Or subscribe for two years for just $12. Call 1-800-992-6656 for a free sample.

With our quarterly magazine, the NOLO *News*, you'll

- **Learn** about important legal changes that affect you
- **Find out first** about new Nolo products
- **Keep current** with practical articles on everyday law
- **Get answers** to your legal questions in *Ask Auntie Nolo's* advice column
- **Save money** with special Subscriber Only discounts
- **Tickle your funny bone** with our famous *Lawyer Joke* column.

OUR NO-HASSLE
GUARANTEE

We've created products we're proud of and
think will serve you well. But if for any reason,
anything you buy from Nolo Press does not
meet your needs, we will refund your purchase price and pay for the cost of returning it
to us by Priority Mail. No ifs, ands or buts.